BUFFALOED

How Race, Gender and Media Bias Fueled a Season of Scandal

D1367622

By
Bruce Plasket

Printed in the United States of America
First Printing 2005

ISBN: 1-59971-025-0

Cover photo courtesy of the University of Colorado Sports Information Department

Back cover photo by Richard Hackett

I dedicate this book to my wife, Julie,
whose faith in me is greater than my own.

Acknowledgments

For their help in producing this book, I would like to acknowledge the University of Colorado football players and their families who allowed me to invade their lives—especially Matt McChesney, Sam Wilder, Ron Monteilh, Bobby Purify and Jesse Wallace. I would like to thank Jimmy Cody, Steve Wojciechowski and all the brave firefighters of New York City for their selfless cooperation. A special thanks to all the University of Colorado employees whose names are not listed here but who cooperated with me at the risk of incurring the wrath of those in Boulder who would silence them. I would also like to acknowledge the support of Howie Eiden, Jeff Fleischman, Trevor Harris, Mike Javernick, Lee Hitchcock, Lori Callahan, Jerry Middleton, Mike Spivey, Mike Tanner, Cydney Tanner (who reminded me of the little in *Remember the Titans*) and all those friends who supported me through both good times and bad.

Contents

Preface... i

Cast of Characters 1

Chapter 1: Buffaloed.. 3

Chapter 2: Boiling Point 10

Chapter 3: Whose Scandal Is It, Anyway? 25

Chapter 4: Up in Here 51

Chapter 5: Day of Infamy 62

Chapter 6: "She Was a Girl" 79

Chapter 7: On the Way Home.. 96

Chapter 8: She Hate Me 112

Chapter 9: Presidents, Governors and Grand Juries 131

Chapter 10: Face Down in a Ditch................................ 151

Chapter 11: Circle the Wagon.. 163

Chapter 12: To Kill a Mockingbird 180

Chapter 13: From the Darkness 197

About the Author

Bruce Plasket has spent most of his adult life in journalism, working at a series of ski-town and small- town newspapers before settling in the Denver area in 1994. Plasket spent the past 10 years covering the federal courts and criminal justice issues for Lehman Newspapers. While there, he led several investigative projects, including a series on a uranium mill that garnered him the Scripps-Howard National Journalism Award and the Society of Environmental Journalists National Award. He has also received numerous awards from a list of professional organizations that includes the Colorado Press Association, The Inland Daily Press Association and the Society of Professional Journalists.

In 2002, while still working as a journalist, Plasket began performing standup comedy at the Comedy Works in Denver and at clubs throughout Colorado. A native of New Jersey, Plasket graduated from the University of Northern Colorado with a Bachelor's degree in political science in 1975. He currently lives in Albuquerque with his wife, dog and bird.

Preface

This is not a book about sports. It is a book primarily about how the media carried the banner for a small group of activists, opportunistic politicians and press agents in creating the perception of a sports scandal in the absence of evidence that a scandal ever happened.

Although I have covered sports in my career, I have for the past 20-plus years covered such stories as the Columbine Massacre, the Oklahoma City bombing case and the JonBenet Ramsey murder in addition to more investigative projects than I can remember.

This story is unlike any of those. While it contains none of the tragic loss of life associated with those other stories, it paints a similar picture of the affects of injustice and hate.

This is a book about race, gender and the media in the context of a college football team's struggle in the face of stereotyping worsened by media bias.

I came about this story and the people in it rather accidentally while covering the federal courts for a newspaper in suburban Denver. It is the story of how the University of Colorado football team and its coach, Gary Barnett, came under a national spotlight because of a scandal fueled by sexism, racism and political opportunism. It is also the story of how 100 young men, most of them black, became the victims of a media blitz caused by unsubstantiated, racially-charged allegations amid an atmosphere regarded as one of the most liberal in America.

This story also shook my own foundation as a lifelong liberal who grew up idolizing Robert Kennedy and who worked for the presidential campaign of George McGovern in 1972. As I uncovered the agendas of those who created this story and made it flourish in the media, I began to believe that some who would be called liberals were guilty of sexism and perhaps even racism in a crusade that quashed the freedom and ruined the reputations of others. Both their words and actions would certainly make Bobby Kennedy roll over in his grave. The thinly-veiled disdain of men exhibited by some of them should sicken both conservatives and liberals who believe in decency and fairness. The politicians and self-absorbed activists in this story seem to me to be hell bent on destroying the multi-racial but male-oriented culture of football and have long since forgotten the liberal tenet that calls for tolerance of other races and cultures. To my surprise, this book exposed me to conservatives who were not bigots and liberals who were, and taught me that the political labels often provide an inaccurate barometer of human decency.

The story follows a group of wrongly-accused young men as they try to shake a reputation heaped on them by a vindictive district attorney, a team of lawyers with a clever press agent and a even a university regent who, in my opinion, ignored the conflict of interest created by her marriage to the attorney whose lawsuit fueled a scandal that was long on expensive investigations and woefully short on evidence.

It is not my purpose to serve as an apologist for or a defender of the University of Colorado, its players or its coach, but rather to expose the forces that have taken advantage of weak reporters who avoided investigating the whole story and whose dereliction has resulted in the destruction of lives, careers and reputations.

Prior to embarking on this story, I had never met Gary Barnett, his players or his assistant coaches. I have since spent a year interviewing, watching and traveling with them and have discovered that they are not the people they have been portrayed to be. I found there to be much more integrity and honor among these men than among the cadre of politically-correct sycophants I had been calling colleagues for so many years. This story digs beneath our stereotyped, snapshot view of football players as cogs in a wheel designed to entertain us for three hours on Saturday. It shows them for who they really are.

It has not been an easy story to uncover or publish. In fact most of this story has, until now, never been reported. During my last year as a reporter I was able to get only portions of it into print, while attitudes and restrictions at both my newspaper and throughout the industry kept the story narrowly focused on the agendas of those with access to the mainstream media while ignoring those who could not defend themselves. After spending 20 years establishing a reputation as a tough, no-holds barred reporter, I found myself being called soft because of my refusal to jump on the bandwagon of bashers and for my insistence on reporting both sides of this complicated story. By the fall of 2004, it was apparent that my journalism career was suffering because of my refusal to go along to get along. I no longer wanted to be included in what I saw as a fraudulent claim of journalistic integrity by my peers.

I had to get out.

Quite simply, this is the story of what I saw and what drove me away from my own profession. Hopefully it will also cause readers and viewers to take a much more critical look at what they are being told by today's news organizations.

Most of the story is written in the third person. Some of it, however couldn't and probably shouldn't be expressed in anyone's words but my own.

It is a story many will not like and one that some will dispute. It is at times ugly and profane. But it is the unvarnished truth that media bias and political correctness have so far stifled. It goes to the root of why I became a journalist—to tell people what really happened.

Oddly, I had to quit being a journalist in order to do that.

Leaving behind a profession I loved was difficult, but what followed quickly became a nightmare. While completing the book in early 2005, I signed a contract with a prominent New York publishing company, which scheduled an August release. In late May, however, that all changed. Shortly after the publishing company announced the publication of the book with a sensational press release – one I didn't like but was in no position to change – it received a letter from Baine Kerr, the attorney who had filed the first Title IX lawsuit alleging that the University of Colorado had used alcohol and ex to attract recruits. Mr. Kerr's six-page letter was accompanied by 54 pages of various court documents and alleged, among other things, that I had violated a federal court order by publishing excerpts of a deposition given by Lisa Simpson, one of the women who had claimed to have been raped at a party attended by football players and recruits. Mr. Kerr has sent a similar letter to my newspaper when I first published the excerpts in early 2004. That assertion flies in the face of the fact that no one in the media was ever under the court order.

That letter also accused me of making "posterboys" of thugs and accused me of demeaning Kerr, his wife (University of Colorado Regent Cindy Carlisle), Boulder County District Attorney Mary Keenan Lacy and Ms. Simpson. He warned the publisher that if the book came out, it would result in a "swamp of litigation." And, he did so without having read the book. His limited knowledge of the book was based on a press release designed to sell books. I reacted to the letter angrily and publicly, stating that Mr. Kerr and his wife were trying to stifle free speech.

Had he read the book before issuing his threats, Mr. Kerr would have known that it doesn't condone rape, doesn't glorify thugs and doesn't sugar-coat wrongdoing by football players or anyone else. It strives to present evidence ignored by reporters who rushed to judgment because of laziness, bias, ineptitude or a combination of those things.

After receiving the letter, however, my publisher's feet got cold very quickly and in June the book and my contract were both cancelled.

I was devastated. The plug had been pulled on the most important story I ever wrote -- one on which I had gambled both my career and my family's future and one I felt compelled to tell if I were to leave journalism with any sense of duty.

As the summer wore on it appeared my book would never see the light of day. A series of publishers passed on it, citing a variety of reasons I saw as polite ways to tell me they were afraid to publish it because of the legal threats. My book had been tainted by accusations made by someone who hadn't even read it.

Mr. Kerr apparently believed I had no right to analyze his actions as a public figure and no right to criticize Ms. Carlisle and Ms. Keenan-Lacy, both elected public officials.

I spent the summer asking myself the same questions over and over.

To what depths would those who had manipulated the media so effectively during the so-called recruiting scandal go in their quest to silence my book?

How could someone use legal threats to silence another's free speech and to interfere with another person's right to make a living?

Why would someone be so afraid of the other side of a story?

By late August it appeared the interference with my contract and the other efforts to stop my book had been successful. It looked as though the cultural war that had created the football scandal would continue to be fought by only one side. But, in late August, I found a publisher.

I stand by the facts in this book. They are the result of more than two years of research and are based on interviews, statements and public records. The opinions expressed here are the product of that research and are mine alone.

This book is not intended to disrespect or demean anyone, including Ms. Simpson. It is an effort to examine the role of gender, race, political correctness and media bias as players in a saga that ended careers, devastated families and falsely painted a group of young men – almost all black – as lawless thugs and rapists.

As a young man I developed the belief that all stories have two sides. As a middle-aged man I have learned that the media is all too often willing to bow to politics, bias and press agents as it shirks its duty to dig beneath mere headlines. Mr. Kerr, Ms. Carlisle and Ms. Keenan-Lacy are all political figures and their efforts to advance their agenda are to be expected.

The media's failure to dig any further in to a story with the potential to ruin lives, however, is not.

It is nothing short of despicable.

At a time when the trustworthiness of the news media is under unprecedented and justifiable attack, this book offers up additional and disturbing evidence that the reporters who were supposed to serve as watchdogs of lawyers, politicians and press agents had instead become their lapdogs.

Writing this story has been one of the most difficult things I've ever done professionally. And it has definitely been the most painful. It would have been much easier to ignore the appalling lack of cynicism exhibited by the reporters whose coverage of this story on both the local and national levels was devoid of balance or fairness.

Many times I have regretted undertaking this project.

But somebody had to do it.

Not doing so would have made me just another lapdog.

It has been said that at some point in life a man, in order to live with himself, has to stand up for something.

For me, that time is now.

Bruce J. Plasket
August 2005

Cast of Characters

Gary Barnett – The 59-year-old coach of the University of Colorado football team, Barnett was temporarily suspended in 2004 after disparaging the football skills of former place-kicker Katie Hnida. During his 30-plus years as a coach, Barnett has been known as a by-the-book disciplinarian, but in 2004 was the subject of several internal and external investigations. None of those investigations produced evidence of wrongdoing.

Cindy Carlisle – University Board of Regents member since 2002, Carlisle is an outspoken critic of the football program, and in 2004 called for a stronger conflict-of-interest policy for the board of regents, in spite of her marriage to Baine Kerr, the attorney for one of the women suing the university.

Regina Cowles – The director of the Boulder chapter of the National Organization for Women, Cowles once accused the university president Elizabeth Hoffman of membership in the "good ol' boys club." In 2002, Cowles worked for Cindy Carlisle during her campaign manager for the board of regents.

Anne Gilmore – A University of Colorado student who initially told a reporter she was not raped at the Simpson party, Gilmore later filed a federal lawsuit claiming she was raped at the party.

Katie Hnida – The only female to ever play football at the University of Colorado and the first woman to ever play in a Division 1 football game, Hnida told *Sports Illustrated* (in 2004) that she was raped by a teammate four years earlier while she was a reserve place-kicker at the school. The alleged incident was never reported to the police, coaches, or university officials.

Mary Keenan – The Boulder district attorney, Keenan helped spark the recruiting controversy with her statement that she believed the University of Colorado football program used sex and alcohol to attract recruits. It was Keenan who charged four black football players with contributing to the delinquency of minors in connection with a party at which two women claimed to have been raped, but who failed to charge white students who admitted supplying alcohol. In 2005, Keenan changed her name to Mary K. Lacy.

Elizabeth Hoffman – The former president of the University of Colorado, Hoffman's term coincided with the scandal. In 2005, Hoffman resigned under heavy criticism for her handling of both the football allegations and the retention of University of Colorado professor Ward Churchill, who authored an essay defending the September 11 terrorist attacks and likened the World Trade Center victims to Nazis.

Ron Monteilh (pronounced mon-táy) – A University of Colorado wide receiver, Ron Monteilh was falsely accused of contributing to the delinquency of a minor at the Simpson party based solely on a faulty photo identification. The charge was later dropped, but Monteilh's reputation continued to suffer.

Lisa Simpson – The host of the December 7, 2001 party, Simpson touched off the recruiting scandal with her lawsuit claiming she was raped by unnamed football players while passed out at the party. Anne Gilmore later joined the suit. It was Simpson press agent Lisa Simon – the former spokeswoman for the family of one of the Columbine High School killers – who distributed Keenan's deposition claiming the university used alcohol and sex to attract recruits.

Bill Owens – The conservative Republican governor of Colorado, Owens referred to the University of Colorado football team as an embarrassment to the state after hearing the liberal Democrat Keenan's accusations that alcohol and sex were being used to recruit players. Owens met for the first time with Gary Barnett in the winter of 2005, but the nature of their meeting remains a secret.

Chapter One
Buffaloed

F ederal judges dismiss civil suits every day, but this was not just any case. It was a case that grabbed national headlines and which produced a perception of a runaway college football program in which sex and alcohol were used as recruiting tools. It was a case that cut a swath through a major university as it swept away careers and reputations.

On March 31, 2005, a federal judge in Denver dismissed a lawsuit claiming the University of Colorado was responsible for the alleged rape of two women by football players and recruits at a 2001 off-campus party.

As it is in most federal court proceedings, U.S. District Judge Robert Blackburn's dismissal of the case was unaccompanied by courtroom drama. There was no CourtTV, no crowd anxiously waiting for a jury to reach a decision. In a move that belied the drama of the previous two years, a clerk merely placed a copy of the judge's order on the front counter in the federal courthouse. The dismissal of the suit created none of the furor created by its filing.

And while the plaintiff's lawyers vowed to appeal the dismissal, the case, at least for the time being, died with barely a whimper after roaring loudly for more than two years and creating a path of destruction that swallowed up lives, careers and reputations.

The suit, filed by CU students Lisa Simpson and Anne Gilmore, was more than an allegation that the two had been raped at a drunken party. It was a broad-brush indictment of the University of Colorado's football program. It claimed CU, using alcohol and sex to attract recruits, used more women than it did towels.

The case also created national headlines and sparked what has been called the biggest scandal in CU football history. Women's groups and victim advocates blasted the school for allowing the football program to run wild. A series of investigations that cost both the university and its athletic department millions of dollars served as stage for those who disliked football and/or men, produced a flood of vague allegations and an even bigger flood of headlines, but no evidence of institutional wrongdoing.

The political fallout was just as heavy. The liberal district attorney in laid-back Boulder flatly stated that unnamed players had committed rape but filed no sex charges and the Republican governor of conservative Colorado called the program an embarrassment to the state.

The scandal eventually led to the forced resignation of CU's athletic director and the retirement of the chancellor. It also resulted in the semi-forced resignation of the school's female president and has been blamed for the transfer of a half-dozen players and the loss of two coaches.

College students have parties every weekend, many very much like the December 2001 party that sparked the CU scandal. It was at that alcohol-and-sex fueled party that co-eds Lisa Simpson and Anne Gilmore claimed to have been raped. Accounts of the party were almost as numerous as the two dozen people who attended, but there was no arguing about some of what happened there.

There was enough alcohol—much of it consumed during a drinking game—to cause one partygoer to throw up on another.

There was some weed being smoked.

And there was a lot of interracial sex.

A subsequent police investigation produced allegations that Simpson was raped by at least two men while she lay in a drunken stupor and that Gilmore awoke from a similar drunken state under a pile of black men. Simpson also told police that several carloads of uninvited football players and the recruits they were entertaining that weekend had crashed the party.

District Attorney Mary Keenan initially charged four players, and eventually a fifth, with felony contribution to the delinquency of a minor. While no rape charges were filed, Keenan publicly insisted that Simpson had been raped and that only "identity problems" precluded prosecution of sex offenses. CU coach Gary Barnett suspended the scholarships of four players and three of them ended up transferring to other schools.

What started as an incident exploded into a full-fledged scandal just over 14 months later when District Attorney Keenan, in a deposition for Simpson's lawsuit, claimed CU used alcohol and sex as recruiting tools. Within days of the release of Keenan's statement, another allegation of sexual assault by an unnamed CU football player surfaced.

Then another.

And another.

The allegations got worse and eventually included a claim by the only female to ever play football at CU that she was raped while on the team. Former place-kicker Katie Hnida, in a February 2004 *Sports Illustrated* article, alleged a teammate had forced himself on her while the two watched TV. She also alleged that her former teammates had subjected her to a series of lewd comments and groping that were part of a constant pattern of sexual harassment. Barnett unwittingly thrust himself into the middle of the firestorm when he told a reporter the other players disrespected Hnida because "she was a girl" and because she was an "awful" kicker.

Barnett's comments turned what had been local TV coverage into ESPN SportsCenter headlines and, within hours of the comments, ashen-faced CU President Elizabeth Hoffman stood before the cameras to announce that Barnett had been suspended and that his job was in jeopardy. While Hoffman shook visibly at that late-night press conference, CU chancellor Richard Byyny looked the part of a beaten man. He sheepishly told reporters that winning and losing "aren't important anymore" and it appeared the CU football program, which had been viewed as among the nation's cleanest under Barnett, was near death.

Byyny would retire within a year and Hoffman would resign shortly thereafter and be replaced by former Republican U.S. Senator Hank Brown. The man who sat Barnett down to tell him of his suspension and possible imminent firing, athletic director Dick Tharp, would resign under pressure before the year's end.

Intelligent observers gave Barnett no chance of surviving a series of investigations into the newly-discovered moral cesspool that was the University of Colorado football program.

But there was a problem with the scandal.

Actually there were a lot of problems.

There were problems with the allegations of Simpson and Gilmore, whose statements were contradicted by friends who said they observed the two engaged in consensual sexual activity with athletes. Other witnesses said Simpson handed out condoms after becoming extremely drunk while playing the drinking game "Power Hour." Gilmore's story seemed to change as time went on. Two days after the party she approached a newspaper columnist and told him of a "gang rape" at the party, but said she was not raped. Gilmore later told police she embellished the story she told the columnist and later admitted engaging in consensual sexual contact with a player. Later, when she filed her own lawsuit, she claimed to have been raped.

There were also problems with the criminal charges. One of the players charged had left the party long before the sexual free-for-all in Simpson's bedroom, but was charged when a recruit he had never met mistakenly identified him in a photo. And, while as many as two dozen minors were drinking at the party, only four black football players were charged. None of the women at the party, all of whom were white, were charged. Neither was the white man who bought alcohol for the women and whose actions were known to law enforcement officials.

There were also questions about Hnida's rape claim. The former kicker admitted that she never told anyone, including the police or her coaches, of the alleged attack until she spoke to columnist Rick Reilly. She also refused to name her alleged assailant, but it was her own alleged conduct that helped make her story suspect. Several witnesses said she joined in crude locker-room humor and had physical relationships with players. While Hnida has denied it, others said her conduct was less than prudent during a bowl game trip.

One of the more disturbing aspects of the case was the Simpson legal team's hiring of the public relations firm which released Keenan's damaging deposition just before the February 2005 TV ratings or "sweeps" period and which served as the source for a myriad of leaked allegations while serving as a spokesman for Simpson. Local victim-advocate and women's organizations lined up behind the publicity generated by the allegations being leaked by Simpson's press agent.

The biggest problem with the scandal, however, had nothing to do with the various characters who seized upon it as part of their own agenda.

It was the media itself. The "problems" with the scandal went unreported amid what to me seemed to be an anti-football, anti-male atmosphere dictated by what I came to believe were the extremists of ultra-liberal Boulder.

No journalist questioned Simpson and Gilmore's stories.

No one asked the DA why the black men had been charged and the white women had not and no one questioned public statements in which she said the players were guilty of rape in the absence of criminal charges.

No one questioned, or even revealed, the fact that Simpson had hired a press agent and that the same press agent was largely responsible for keeping the story hot.

No one investigated Hnida's time at CU.

Not one reporter questioned the possible conflict of interest on the part of CU Regent Cindy Carlisle, who is married to Simpson's attorney and who was elected to the university's governing board three weeks before her husband filed the suit. And reporters sat silent when Carlisle questioned the makeup of a committee formed to investigate the recruiting allegations. Reporters allowed themselves to be spoon-fed by special interests and failed to ask questions.

The media had lost its cynicism.

But it hadn't lost its aggression.

Reporters worked overtime looking for more allegations. Victim advocates and the DA were quick to provide nebulous charges that came with no names and no evidence, and those allegations found their way into print and on the air. When CU players found themselves the victims of racially-fueled threats, those threats went unreported.

Suddenly it was politically incorrect to question any allegation of sex assault. It was wrong to ask questions. It was okay to ignore racial hate crimes against football players. And the ethical requirement of reporting both sides of the story had just as suddenly disappeared. Columnists in Colorado and across the country called for Barnett's head under the assumption that the allegations were true.

In the vacuum created by inept media, politicians and press agents decided what was news, dictating the coverage of an event that would shatter the lives of many innocent people. A small group of extremists had hijacked the feminist movement in Colorado and had overtaken the media without so much as a fight, allowing the Simpson-Gilmore lawyers to try their case against CU in the court of public opinion.

Political correctness became more important than factual correctness while racism and sexism undermined the credibility of and the horrific pain suffered by rape victims.

An endless series of investigations and audits, meanwhile, found no substance to allegations that Barnett and his staff knew about or condoned sex assault or subjugation of women. Money legally earned by Barnett and legally spent on his football camps turned into a "slush fund" in the news, while sealed grand jury reports and financial audits found their way to reporters who wouldn't know a slush fund if they stepped in one. Those who broke the law in releasing that self-serving, sealed information were never prosecuted.

Whether or not the Simpson-Gilmore suit is revived in the appellate courts, its effect will be felt for years. Players branded as rapists will carry that taint for the rest of their lives.

While surrendering their independence to the political correctness police, reporters missed a very important fact about the CU scandal.

Their conduct was the only real scandal. They trumpeted unsubstantiated allegations, failed to investigate those charges and later crawled under a rock—failing to follow up their sensational stories after numerous official investigations found the scandal to be virtually without substance. There was virtually no news coverage and not a single apology from law enforcement or the media when charges against a player were dropped months after it became apparent that he was mistakenly identified by someone he had never met.

The media's scandalous conduct demonized the University of Colorado football team as it entered the 2004 season with roads trips to some already-hostile locales. I witnessed that season first-hand and from the inside. This is the story of both the politically-fueled scandal and the season that followed.

Chapter Two
Boiling Point

In spite of the fact that he would be voted the team's Best Interview by local sportswriters, Matt McChesney spoke to reporters only on his coach's orders. Given the beating his team had taken, he hated talking to the reporters he had come to loath in the past year.

In the locker room, however, he rarely stopped talking

The 6-6, 290-pound senior defensive tackle was the colorful, often profane vocal leader of the embattled University of Colorado football team—a local boy who attended high school five miles from Boulder and never considered playing college ball anywhere else.

Adorned in a black do-rag, a thinly-trimmed beard and an assortment of knee and elbow braces, the fifth-year senior would wave his massive, tattooed arms as he exhorted his teammates.

"Let's whup that ass and go home," he would bellow from the depths of the stadium before his team's road game with Washington State. McChesney wasn't much for putting his feelings and words through the filter of political correctness. For me, it was refreshing to see that locker rooms are one of the few remaining places where the First Amendment isn't filtered through someone else's idea of what is appropriate. For McChesney, that was a good thing.

"I'm gonna go out there and fuck somebody up," he would yell in the locker room before the Nebraska game.

When McChesney spoke, the other players listened. With what his coach would call the "heart and soul" of the team, he spoke often. But under the heavy fog that obscured the Omni Interlocken Hotel on Sept. 4, 2004, McChesney wasn't saying anything. Neither was anyone else. The hotel where the CU Buffaloes spent their pre-game nights was surprisingly quiet.

Families of some of the players ate breakfast in the hotel restaurant as the fog kept the hotel invisible from the Denver-Boulder Turnpike just a couple hundred yards away. In a meeting room across the hall from where the team's weekly chapel service was set to begin at 9 a.m., coach Gary Barnett drank coffee with a handful of players and coaches while watching the first ESPN pre-game show of the season. A few of the players read the sports section from a stack of free copies of the *Boulder Daily Camera* newspapers that had been left in the room.

"It will be tough for embattled CU coach Gary Barnett," the ESPN Gameday host said.

"Embattled," Barnett repeated to himself with a faint smirk. To the rest of the world, however, he was, indeed, embattled. Barnett had earlier that year been accused of using alcohol and sex to attract recruits and accused of covering for a player accused of assaulting a female trainer. He had also been suspended for three months after referring to former kicker Katie Hnida's abilities as "awful" and "terrible" after she accused an unnamed teammate of raping her nearly five years earlier. During that suspension Barnett took a media relations course designed to keep him from answering questions such as the one about Hnida's skill as a kicker. Even Barnett supporters who agreed with his assessment of Hnida's talent considered his comments to be ill-advised. Now he sipped coffee only hours away from his first post-game interview of a new season that would bring more scrutiny of his every word and deed. Running back Lawrence Vickers, the one player almost as outspoken as McChesney, sang along out loud to the music blaring in his headphones as he stared at the TV in the meeting room.

Minutes later, the team chaplain, former CU and NFL cornerback Mike Spivey, would bring up the subject that had gone unmentioned all morning.

"Everything they said about you was a lie," he preached to

the room full of players dressed in black travel sweats. "They want to make every man in this room invisible, but you guys are building great things. You must tell yourself, 'Tonight I will not hide'."

For the previous seven months, CU's players had plenty of reasons to hide. They had become the public scourge of the college football world—the poster children for all that was wrong with college athletics.

It began with the claims by Lisa Simpson and Anne Gilmore that they had been raped at a 2001 party attended by both players and recruits. Then Boulder District Attorney Mary Keenan, in a deposition for the Simpson suit, claimed CU used alcohol and sex to attract recruits. Within weeks of the release of Keenan's comments, Denver TV stations, with the newspapers following behind them, would say that six—and later nine—mostly unnamed women had accused unnamed players of rape. By 2005 the number of rapes of unnamed women by unnamed football players had somehow risen to 10, although none were accompanied by evidence. Those numbers, many of which were supplied by victim advocates who refused to elaborate on the circumstances of the alleged attacks or provide documentation, went unquestioned by the media.

While she did not file a lawsuit, Hnida's rape claim, combined with Barnett's politically-incorrect answer to a reporter's repeated question, formed a flash point in the repeated attacks on Barnett's character and the program. For many it added credence to allegations that Barnett was insensitive to sexual assault and didn't respect women. Hnida's story compounded and seemed to validate the stories of the other accusers and provided the scandal with its first national stage. The sheer volume of those collective allegations seemed to add to the credibility of each one individually. In a February 23, 2004 piece by *Sports Illustrated* humor columnist Rick Reilly, Hnida claimed to have been sexually harassed by the male players and, in August of 2000, raped by a teammate. The next day Barnett's comment—the one he made after repeated questions from a reporter about Hnida not being a good kicker—would draw him a suspension that would last through spring football practice. By the time the spring drills began without the head coach, CU had become, in the eyes of the media, a cesspool.

CU was suddenly a place where football recruits were supplied with alcohol and sex.

A place where women who refused the advances of athletes were raped.

A place where the football coach didn't care if a female player was raped.

The events at CU even united politicians from both ends of the spectrum. When Colorado Governor Bill Owens, a Republican, heard of the accusations by Keenan, a Democrat, he put their political differences aside long enough to agree with her.

"The CU football team is an embarrassment to the state," he said. Two years earlier, Owens' own ill-advised comments had gotten him in hot water with the tourism industry when, in the wake of a series of wildfires, he told reporters, "The whole state is on fire." In fact, only a few places were on fire and, politically speaking, so were the governor's pants.

While CU was disturbingly assumed guilty of all sorts of ill behavior, no one was asking the disturbing questions about the roles of race, gender and politics in the CU scandal. Why were all the defendants black? Was there a possibility the charges were false? Whose agenda was driving the story? DA Keenan, who was a deputy prosecutor during the JonBenet Ramsey debacle and who had been elected DA in 2000, had charged four black football players with contributing to the delinquency of a minor by bringing alcohol and/or marijuana to the party where Simpson and Gilmore had claimed to have been raped. Records show the underage white women who admitted drinking or supplying alcohol were not charged. Neither was the 21-year-old white man who, in a deposition in the Simpson suit, admitting buying beer for them—an instance of contributing to minors that was ignored.

One of the black football players, wide receiver Ron Monteilh, was charged with a felony based on a mistaken photo identification made by a recruit who had never met him. That charge was later quietly dropped, but the dismissal received almost no play in the media. During the off season, five players—three of them black—had transferred to other schools. The accusations straddled CU with the dual challenges of keeping its own black players from transferring away from what they saw as an increasingly anti-black atmosphere and attracting other black athletes to the program. Barnett's job uncertainty wasn't helping the recruiting process, either.

By the time practice started in August, football was nearly the last thing on the minds of those who followed CU. Although an independent committee investigation and a grand jury probe had produced no evidence of wrongdoing, the program, from the outside, appeared to be near ruin. Barnett and his "Buffs" were out to dispel that notion, but they were heavy underdogs in that quest.

As the sun melted the fog outside the hotel on that early September day, McChesney led the way as the players, many with headphones on, silently filed out of the hotel to fill the three shiny new buses that would take them on the 10-mile ride to Folsom Field in Boulder. A quiet tension mounted as the buses, adorned with CU logos and flanked by Colorado State Patrol cars with lights flashing and sirens waling, made their way through the fog and up the turnpike. While they said nothing, the players had to have been wondering what sort of reception they would receive in their home stadium in their first season following the winter of their discontent. The coaches had tried to keep the players' minds only on football and the next three months would test their ability to do so.

"Don't listen to the haters," McChesney had told his teammates earlier in the week. As it turned out, there were no "haters" to be found that day. As the motorcade pulled onto the turnpike, horns honked. Fists pointed out car windows in solidarity. When the buses rolled by the Coal Creek Golf Course south of Boulder, a group of golfers dropped their clubs and saluted the motorcade—holding their salutes until the buses went by. CU's fans appeared to be solidly behind the players in spite of what had been written and broadcast about them.

Although all were dressed alike in black sweat suits, the players on those buses represented a wide range of backgrounds and ethnicities.

Offensive tackle Clint O'Neal grew up on a large dairy farm near Weatherford, Texas, and planned to return to the farming life when his football career was over.

Linebacker Jordan Dizon, who was about to start at linebacker in his first college game, was only three months removed from the westernmost high school in the United States on the island of Kauai, Hawaii. While growing up, Dizon hunted wild boar armed with nothing but a knife.

Running back Bobby Purify, the nephew of former NFL wide receiver Webster Slaughter, was a Colorado kid who played on a state basketball championship team at Palmer High School in Colorado Springs. He was also the grandson of Bobby Purify, who, along with his cousin James Purify, recorded the mid-1960s hits, "I'm Your Puppet" and "Shake Yer Tailfeather."

Senior guard Terrance Barreau, who would be nearly 25 years old before playing his last college game of his senior year, had attended the United States Air Force Academy and served two years of active duty in the Air Force before coming to CU.

Linebacker Joe Sanders was the son of a preacher. So was cornerback Chris Russell, whose father, David, preached at a small church in Nashville, Tennessee, and worked part-time as a janitor to support his family. Many others, like Monteilh, had been raised by single mothers in rough neighborhoods.

While the players rode the bus, many of their parents were already in Boulder. Some could afford to fly to every game, while others drove or took buses to games close to their homes. This day would bring an unusually high number of parents anxious to see the first game their sons would play after the scandalous off season.

When the motorcade of buses reached Boulder hundreds of people lined the route, cheering as if the past seven months had never happened. When the team pulled off Stadium Drive at the statue of Olympic marathon runner Frank Shorter up to the side gate at Folsom Field, a tunnel of about 1,000 fans surrounded the players as they walked to the locker room. Absent were the protest signs and demonstrators that had accompanied the May news conference announcing Barnett's reinstatement.

At least for today, the sun had burned off the fog for the CU football team, both literally and figuratively.

For three hours on Saturday, the Buffaloes were heroes in Boulder, the place where only months before a cultural war nearly destroyed football at the University of Colorado. As the season began there were questions as to whether or not the program would survive and those questions would linger after the season's end. Both the University of Colorado football team and Boulder were likely to be in the news for a long time.

It wasn't like Boulder hadn't been in subject of national headlines before. What became known as the CU recruiting scandal didn't mark the first time Boulder had been the butt of jokes. If comedians had to pay royalties every time they made fun of Boulder, the beautiful little city 24 miles north of Denver would be able to buy each of its residents a new Land Rover.

Or a second one.

Making fun of Boulder became a near-national pastime in the

mid 1990s during the JonBenet Ramsey murder case, as late-night talk-show hosts made a living ridiculing the way the Boulder Police bungled the case. That bungling began when a detective, by her own admission, tainted the crime-scene evidence by placing a blanket over the little girl's body and by allowing several people to walk through the scene repeatedly. It continued with public spats between police determined to focus on JonBenet's parents and prosecutors determined to look at other suspects. The case, not surprisingly, was never solved and has found its way to what appears to be a permanent back shelf in the office of District Attorney Mary Keenan.

Boulder, perhaps the most politically-correct city in America, had often made itself an easy target for critics and comedians. Years after it became one of the first cities in America to list its elevation in meters, not feet, Boulder changed its municipal code to remove use of the word "pet" in its animal codes. "Pet" was replaced with the phrase "animal companion." The explanation was that the word "pet" indicated ownership, not companionship, and that ownership was somehow de-humanizing to animals.

Some years ago Boulder changed its "Dead End" street signs to read "No Outlet," since "Dead End" was believed to carry a negative connotation. There was no such concern for the dead-ended Ramsey investigation. In the late 1990s a Boulder city councilman floated the idea of reducing automobile traffic by tracking cars with cameras attached to traffic lights and taxing people who drove too much. Another wanted to ban driving altogether on Wednesdays. Yet another council member once tried to introduce an ordinance that would limit public gatherings to 15 minutes, a measure that would give police the power to roust the dirty, panhandling street people on the Pearl Street Mall. The city attorney's office mercifully informed the council that the ordinance would infringe upon the constitutionally-guaranteed right to free assembly and would certainly be overturned. The law never came to a vote.

Ordinances such as the one that dictates which plants and flowers can be planted in private yards add to Boulder's reputation as an oppressive, elitist upscale college town where "Free Tibet" bumper stickers are as numerous as hiking boots. The city that used to pride itself on its tolerance of free thought seems to have succumbed to a majority-tyranny that has made it quite the opposite.

For a city whose economy was once fueled by the rich cocaine trade of the 1970s and which serves as an unofficial, underground mecca for the North American Man-Boy Love Association—a group of men who believe pedophilia should be legalized—Boulder has a pretty high opinion of itself. Detractors have called it "20 Square Miles Surrounded by Reality," "The People's Republic of Boulder," and the "Berkeley of the Rockies." The 18-mile long Denver-Boulder Turnpike has been called "The Disorient Expressway."

Boulder's 100,000 residents are largely affluent and nearly all white. According to the Bureau of Census (2002) 86 percent are Caucasian and 42 percent of all citizens have a bachelors or graduate college degree. Their majestic homes sit under giant trees. Real estate prices are high. The Porsche dealership is located next to the Sylvan Learning Center. Dread-locked, upper-middle-class white kids known as "Trustafarians" hang around the two-block area across from the campus known as the Hill.

There is also a certain pressure to conform to the stereotypical Boulder lifestyle. Several years ago a Boulder man unsuccessfully tried to get the city to make his neighbor stop barbecuing in his yard. It seems the complaining neighbor found the smell of meat to be nauseating and repugnant because he was a vegetarian. Another Boulder man has taken it upon himself to follow dogs and their owners on the county's expansive open space areas, collecting the dog excrement not picked up by owners as required by county. This crusading man then follows or tracks the owners to their homes, where he delivers both the dog doo and a stern lecture about picking up after one's dog. He also reports the scofflaw dog owners to authorities. Now there's a social crusade for the New Millennium. In Boulder that man is known as an activist. In most cities he would be known as a fool.

For years, the culture of the city known as the Berkeley of the Rockies had co-existed with the football culture of a program that had produced a national championship in the 1990 season and which had fed the National Football League with dozens of players. In 2004, those worlds collided. Football Boulder and Bierkenstock Boulder clashed as they never had before in a battle that had simmered since the time when illicit drug sellers openly hawked their wares on sidewalks only blocks from the campus football factory.

During their training camp in August, the CU football players repeatedly said they just wanted to play football. On the outside they acted as if they thought the scandalous allegations were none of their concern and they never spoke of them unless asked. It was as if success on the field would prove they were innocent of the allegations leveled against them. But the beginning of football practice hadn't changed the media's preoccupation with the off-field stories. The team's August media day, normally attended by only a handful of local beat writers, had become a national affair. *The New York Times* sent a reporter. ESPN.com sent its new college football writer, Pat Forde, who had played for Barnett during his senior year at Air Academy High School near Colorado Springs. Forde, who remembered Barnett as a strict disciplinarian, scratched his head at the allegations of a program gone wild. "He used to bust guys for holding hands in the hallways (with their girlfriends)," Forde said of his old coach.

Even *Sport Illustrated*, which originated the Katie Hnida rape story, sent a reporter to practice. But it wasn't Rick Reilly, the columnist who wrote the story and who was not real popular among the CU players and coaches. "I'm from *Sports Illustrated*," the young woman told the graduate assistant who controlled access to the practice field and who kept a list of approved guests on a clipboard.

"You aren't on the list," intern coach Hunter Hughes politely told her. "You have to check in with the sports information office."

The program's relationship with the media, while civil on the surface, was wrought with unspoken tension. In the weeks leading up to the 2004 season players avoided reporters when possible, while coaches and the sports information department seemed to endure, rather than embrace, reporters. On the Monday before the opening game against Colorado State University, sports information director David Plati cut off questions after an Associated Press reporter asked McChesney, "Do you have any black friends?" While the players rarely spoke of the scandal, it was clear they had no use for reporters. McChesney would later say he couldn't stand the media and only spoke to reporters "because GB (his nickname for Barnett) asked me to."

To say the off-season allegations had created a bunker mentality among the CU players would be an understatement. Barnett and his staff had milked the us-against-the-world theme for all it was worth. He frequently used the words "team on a mission" and called the 2004 squad the closest-knit group he had ever coached. When the team gathered for training camp in early August, he described the atmosphere in the team auditorium as "electric."

Joel Klatt, the 22-year-old quarterback who had played minor league baseball for two years and who had two years of eligibility remaining, had either emerged or had been designated as the team's public spokesman. The religious Klatt, who spends most of his off time attending or speaking to religious functions and who in September 2004 would join Purify in serving the squeaky-clean role of grand marshal of the Oktoberfest Parade in nearby Longmont, gave all the right answers and always kept his cool with reporters. Privately, however, Klatt shared his teammates' distrust of the media. "We've had to shut up for seven months," he told his teammates before the opening game of the 2004 season. "Now we get to make our statement."

Opening day had been a long day of waiting for the Buffs. During breakfast at the team hotel, defensive end James Garee, who at breakfast was as wound up as Tom Arnold at Starbucks, said he preferred to play earlier in the day. "There's nothing to do all day when you play at night," he said. Few people outside the team knew that Garee's father, Jack, was battling terminal cancer. Fellow defensive end Abraham Wright, a recent junior-college transfer, busied himself reading the Bible. While the players stuffed themselves with eggs, ham, bacon and pancakes, Barnett ate only a bowl of oatmeal.

"Where were you at chapel this morning?" he joked to Wright.

"I got up and read my Bible and prayed," Wright responded.

As if to give them something to do during the day-long wait, the coaches put the players through a 10:30 a.m. "walk-through" practice on the lawn outside the hotel. Lunch was served as 2 p.m. At 3:15 p.m. the offense and defense met separately. At 3:25 the defensive players joined the offense in the last meeting before the trip to the stadium. The offensive players clapped in unison as the defensive players entered the room. After a short meeting, the players were told to be on the buses by 3:35 p.m. There was no need for the order. The anxious players were all on the bus within a minute of the meeting's end.

The previous night—like the previous seven months—had seemed like an eternity. Before heading for the hotel, the players gathered in the 100-seat auditorium next to their locker room. From the theater seats above the stage, they heard Barnett urge them to be "the best team for three hours on Saturday." It was the first of many times he would deliver that message. Barnett also read through a copy of the team itinerary each player had been handed on his way to the meeting. The cover of the itinerary handout bore the phrase "212 degrees. Boiling Point." The sixth-year head coach's attempt to transform his team's anger and frustration into game-time intensity was obvious as he explained the difference between passion and emotion. Too much emotion will cause mistakes, he warned. Passion will prevent them. Barnett's voice rose to a football-coach bellow only a few times as he reeled off a few last-minute rules.

"No do-rags on the bus."

"No visitors in the hotel except on the first floor. No visitors upstairs."

Then Barnett's voice began to rise. "We are at a boiling point," he said over the reading glasses that hung on the end of his nose and made him look more like a 58-year-old history professor than a football coach.

Prior to an evening meal of prime rib, lasagna and chicken on the eve of their first game, the players followed special-teams meetings with a one-hour, no-pads practice in an empty Folsom Field. Barnett sat on the west sideline, taping his pre-game show with KOA radio play-by announcer Mark Johnson, who had joined the station during the off season. A few yards away Joel Meyers, who would do the play-by-play for Fox Sports Television's coverage the next day, remembered growing up near Chesterfied, Missouri, the St. Louis suburb where Barnett attended high school. "Barnett went to Parkway Central," he said. "They were a big rival." As he looked around the stadium, he marveled at the beauty of Boulder. "They could have put us in a better hotel, though," he said.

When Meyers returned to Folsom Field the next day, it was full and loud.

Barnett was all smiles by the time the team walked through the tunnel of fans a full two hours before the 6:10 p.m. kickoff dictated by Fox Sports, which was televising the game. While Barnett high-fived fans, the wide-eyed players seemed surprised by the outpouring of support. Inside the locker room, they began the long process of taping up, stretching and strapping on their pads. In groups, the players made their way out onto the surface of Folsom Field. The pre-game rituals were detailed and planned down to the minute.

5:02 p.m. Punters, kickers, snappers, holders and kick returners to the field.

5:07 p.m. Quarterbacks to the field.

5:12 p.m. Centers to the field.

5:17 p.m. Wide receivers, tight ends, running backs and defensive backs to the field.

5:32 p.m. Team stretch.

5:35 p.m. Warm up.

5:48 p.m. Field goal warm-up.

5:49 p.m. Punt warm-up.

Just before 6 p.m. the team left the field and headed back to the auditorium. Some paced silently or sat alone staring at the floor. Others prayed alone or with other players. Occasional shouts of encouragement broke the silence. Two minutes before what was perhaps the most anticipated "walk out" in the team's history, Barnett gathered the team and reminded them of the things he earlier said he didn't have to remind them about. Former wide receiver-kick returner Jeremy Bloom, who had been denied eligibility by the NCAA because he had become a professional skier, had returned from his ski training in Chile to be with his former teammates and was sitting in the back of the auditorium. The air was thick as Barnett noticed Bloom in the back row.

"Bloom, do you have anything to say?" he asked.

"I love you guys. You are my brothers," Bloom said. "Now go out there and kick CSU's fuckin' ass."

Barnett, who rarely swears, seemed taken aback.

"Thanks, Bloom," he said.

Team chaplain Mike Spivey, who never swears, didn't bat an eye.

Emotions started to boil over as the team gathered at the door that leads out to the field. The players were jumping up and down and getting louder. A machine that created the smoke at the team-exit door made vision impossible in the narrow hallway as the smoke billowed back into the building. This was a moment of reckoning for Colorado, which, after winning the Big 12 North in both 2001 and 2002, had slipped to a 5-7 record in 2003. A team that had risen to Number 3 in the national polls in 2001 with the nation's best running attack, the Buffaloes had finished the 2003 season ranked 113th among 117 Division One teams in rushing. During the disappointing 2003 season the team also lost star tailback Bobby Purify to an ankle injury. The soft-spoken Purify had been given a medical redshirt and was anxious to make his mark in this, his senior year.

As the team came out onto the floor of sold-out Folsom Field, Barnett stopped to give the contractually-obligatory 30-second interview to Fox sideline reporter Jim Knox. Predictably, Knox questioned the effect of the scandal on the team. Barnett, just as predictably, said his team was just happy to be back on the field. "I don't want to waste a minute of it," he told Knox in a voice that seemed to wonder how long he would be around. "We're just going to go out and play." Asked if he thought his team might be "too pumped up" emotionally, Barnett said, "There's nothing we can do about it now."

Although Colorado State won the coin toss, it deferred to CU in order to get the ball at the opening of the second half. After receiving the kickoff that ended its most trying off-season ever, the Buffaloes played like they had something to prove.

So did Purify. On the first play of the game, Purify was tackled for a 1-yard loss. On the second play Ron Monteilh, the receiver who had been wrongfully accused of rape seven months before, caught a 3-yard pass. But it was Purify, who had put on 20 pounds in the off season, who led CU on an 80-yard, 10-play drive that ended with him scoring a 1-yard touchdown that put the Buffs up 7-0. On its second possession, CU went 63 yards on 12 plays before Klatt scored from the 1-yard-line to make it 14-0. In the second quarter, sophomore kicker Mason Crosby kicked a 31-yard field goal and CU went up 17-0. Purify finished the first half with 110 rushing yards, but Colorado State scored a touchdown with 23 seconds left in the first half to make the score 17-7.

Inside the auditorium at halftime, while assistant trainers walked around with cups of Gatorade, Barnett would tell his team that only a couple of penalties had kept them from dominating their in-state rival. Offensive line coach Dave Borberly lined his players up in chairs facing the giant blackboard behind the stage and began scribbling adjustments on the black board while the defense met in the next room. "Keep it up," someone yelled as the defensive players re-entered the room. With the exception of that last drive, CU had dominated its rival. But CSU, which had beaten Barnett's team three times in the five seasons he had been CU's coach, had other ideas.

Colorado State and former CU running back Marcus Houston, whose acrimonious transfer from CU two years earlier hadn't been forgotten by the members of either team, came back strong in the third quarter. Houston, who was listed as CSU's third-or fourth-string tailback, had surprisingly been chosen to start the game against CU. The bad blood was evident. Houston, who had gained a nearly-unheard of sixth year of eligibility from the NCAA after leaving CU, become a pariah among his former teammates after his departure, which was marked by allegations that former CU running backs coach Eric Bienemy had questioned his toughness and referred to him as "Markeesha." Houston, who seemed to exchange words with CU defenders each time he was tackled, scored on a 1-yard run with 8:43 left in the third quarter to bring his team within three points. CSU finished washing away CU's early domination when Jeff Babcock kicked a 26-yard field goal to tie the game at 17 with 11:42 left in the fourth quarter.

Crosby awakened the crowd with 6:43 left in the game when he kicked a 55-yard field goal to put CU up 20-17 and linebacker Brian Iwuh appeared to seal the game on CSU's next play when he intercepted CSU quarterback Justin Holland and returned the ball for a 37-yard touchdown to give CU a seemingly insurmountable 27-17 lead.

Holland, whose flamboyant predecessor Bradlee VanPelt had infuriated CU fans with pre-game trash talk the previous three years, wasn't yet finished. With 4:35 left in the game, he threw a 31-yard pass to Johnny Walker to once again bring his team within 3 points at 27-24. CU was forced to punt on its last possession and CSU had one last chance to end the Buffs' storybook return from its nightmare off season.

With seconds remaining in the game, CSU was inside the CU 10-yard line and the game seemed to be headed for overtime if the Rams could manage a field goal. A touchdown would break CU's back and its heart. With time for two plays before the clock ran out, CSU coach Sonny Lubick disdained the field goal with his team at CU's 1-yard line. Houston ran the ball, but was stopped for no gain. On the final play—one that both Lubick and Holland would later attribute to confusion—Holland handed the ball to running back Tristen Walker, who was considered physically stronger than Houston. CU safety J.J. Billingsley, remembering what secondary coach Craig Bray had told him numerous times during the week, read the keys and recognized the play. He ran Walker down and, with help from safety Dominique Brooks, dropped him for a 2-yard loss as the clock ran out.

CU had escaped with a 27-24 win in the waning days of summer. Still hanging over the program, however, were the allegations that had blindsided the program. That didn't seem to faze the thousands of students who poured out of the stands to join a mid-field celebration. A moment of victory had at least temporarily cleansed the collective soul of the CU football program. Up in the press box, skeptical reporters said the Buffs had been lucky their defense and special teams had gotten their anemic offense off the hook. It was a theme that would be repeated in the press box and in print for the next three months.

At game's end, Purify and some of the other players began a strange ritual that would be held as a closely-guarded secret until the end of the season. Acting on an idea concocted over the summer by senior defensive tackle Brandon Dabdoub, the players, after a win, would pour a small amount of sand from a bottle they had filled in August. The pouring of the sand was meant to symbolize a gradual exorcising of the team's off-season problems.

Pouring a few grains of sand on Folsom Field after one win was a good start to the youthful superstition, but the Buffs would soon realize that sand is easier to collect than wins in the Big 12 Conference and that ritual does not wash away stigma. The pouring of the sand, as odd as it appeared, seemed somehow appropriate. It was reminiscent of the introduction to "The Days of Our Lives," the long-running soap that features sand running through an hourglass. The players' lives had been a soap opera for the past seven months, and the next three months would bring even more drama to the days of their young lives.

I had no idea the level to which that drama was about to be taken, but had a close-up view of the drama that proceeded the 2004 season. I had covered what had become known as the CU scandal since its inception, but when the scandal broke in its full force in February of 2004 I began to investigate how those events unfolded and who had caused them to come to light. That process started when I tracked down CU coach Gary Barnett after he had called out the media on a radio talk show. I wasn't ready for what I was about to find.

Chapter Three
Whose Scandal Is It, Anyway?

A s a rule, radio sports talk shows drive me crazy.
That's why my alarm clock is set to a local sports station.

Five minutes of mindless blather is usually enough to roust me from my bed. On a cold February morning in 2004, however, one of those early-morning sportslobotomy shows triggered a series of events that would change the way I thought about my career as a journalist and which would eventually cause me to lose respect for the business to which I have dedicated most of my adult life.

"We'll have University of Colorado football coach Gary Barnett when we return after these messages," bellowed Lou From Littleton, the morning guy on Denver's KKFN.

I'd better listen to this, I thought. Barnett and his program had become the biggest story in the state and one of the biggest sports stories in the country. Rarely did an hour pass on the local radio sports-talk shows without extensive discussion of the CU situation. Newspaper columnists were already calling for his firing. While I had never met Barnett, he had, in the past two weeks, become perhaps the most famous football coach in America. As part of my job covering the federal court in Denver, I had been, since late 2002, writing about two lawsuits in which two co-eds had alleged they had been raped at a December 2001 party attended by CU football players and recruits. The allegations in the lawsuit were disturbing and painted a picture of a football program out of control. I, like everyone else who read the allegations in the suit without further scrutiny, was ready to assume Barnett's players were little more than libidinous thugs and that he had turned a blind eye to their behavior. It looked bad.

In early 2004, the news got worse for CU.

In a deposition given as part of one of the lawsuits and given to me by the co-eds' press agent, Boulder District Attorney Mary Keenan accused the CU football program of "using alcohol and sex to attract recruits."

With that explosive bit of information, I—along with my colleagues in Colorado and across the country—was off to the races.

Barnett immediately and vehemently denied the allegations, but his defense was limited. Hours after Keenan's allegations found their way to Denver's top-rated TV news station on the eve of the all-important February sweeps or rating period, Barnett and everyone else at the school were largely muzzled and the standard "We don't comment on pending litigation" answer was in full use. The TV stations, that set their advertising rates on audience figures gathered during the February and May ratings periods, later denied allegations of a sweeps-month feeding frenzy. Barnett was free to deny the allegations in general terms, but refrained from addressing them specifically. Both the university and its football coach had been painted into a corner that made them targets for a series of allegations against which they could not defend themselves.

Given the school's tight-lipped policy, I was surprised to hear Barnett on the radio that February morning. He was in a fighting mood.

"I'd like to challenge every so-called investigative journalist in this town to look at the whole picture and tell the whole story," he blurted out without hinting what those journalists might find.

I bolted up in bed.

Who is this guy, I asked myself. I've been an investigative reporter for 20 years and here he is challenging my competence. I made my way to my computer, found Barnett's e-mail address and wrote him a short message in which I accepted his challenge. I told him that if he wanted facts, I would find them and that I wouldn't sugarcoat anything for him, the DA or anyone else. I left him my phone number but didn't expect to ever hear from him.

I was wrong.

Three hours later my phone rang. It was Barnett, the guy I had never met but, because of the lawsuit's allegations of intolerable conduct, was primed to dislike.

"We just want someone to be fair to us, give us a chance," he said. "Find all the facts and report them, no matter where the chips fall. We have nothing to hide."

This guy is either innocent or crazy, I thought. Not since Gary Hart challenged the Miami Herald to follow him had anyone thrown down such an ill-advised gauntlet, I reasoned. Extensive research into his background and interviews with people who had known him for decades told me Barnett had always been known as a strict disciplinarian and a straight arrow. He was, simply put, a square. Events since then seem to back up that characterization. A series of investigations failed to find him guilty of any ethical or moral wrongdoing and innocent of any NCAA violations in connection with the "recruiting scandal," but that doesn't seem to have helped the now-tarnished public perception of him. A university investigative committee report, the district attorney's probe, a grand jury and a financial audit have been completed without finding that Barnett broke the law or the university's rules. In the spring of 2004 a second audit conducted by State of Colorado and an Internal Revenue Service investigation into Barnett's football camps were also launched and Barnett again predicted that nothing irregular would be found.

At the end of my first conversation with Barnett, I agreed to read copies of the 2,000 pages of investigative reports, statements and depositions generated by the 2001 party and the subsequent lawsuits. I agreed to interview people who had so far been ignored.

"I'll get back to you," I told Barnett.

I spent the next 11 days virtually locked in my house—poring over public documents anyone could have obtained for 15 cents a page and some depositions that, according to some, I wasn't supposed to have. Several copies of those depositions were floating around—and could be legally obtained – before parts of some of them they were sealed by a federal judge in early 2004. The order that sealed those documents applied only to parties in the suit, not the media.

What I found during my examination of that pile of documents answered many of the questions I had asked myself two weeks earlier, when the CU situation inexplicably went from being a minor story to a major national scandal overnight.

During those 11 days I discovered that I—and every reporter in town—had seen and reported on only a portion of the scandal story. We were unwittingly becoming both a part of the scandal and a major factor in the lawsuits by covering, at best, half of the story. What I uncovered was indeed scandalous.

But not for CU.

It was a black mark on law enforcement, the mindless political correctness of Boulder, a vindictive female district attorney and, most disturbingly for me, my fellow reporters.

What was being called a scandal, I realized, was rooted in our willingness as reporters to be spoon-fed by press agents who provided only juicy details that bolstered their case, cut off those who didn't go along for the ride and who tried to hide information that disturbed their agenda.

After digging for a few days, I called Barnett back.

"You were right," I said. "There's something very wrong here. All of us (reporters) have been used." Two weeks earlier, I would have sworn something like that could never happen. The events that bewildered me weeks before were starting to make some sense.

They were also starting to make me mad.

In late January it's difficult to find sports news that doesn't have something to do with the Super Bowl. When it comes to media attention, it's hard to compete with what has become the single biggest sporting event in America. In the days leading up to Super Bowl XXXVIII, the college football team that plays in the shadow of the Rocky Mountains and in the even bigger shadow of the locally-revered Denver Broncos stole the national spotlight when a lawsuit that had operated under the media radar for over a year suddenly became what would be one of the biggest sports stories of 2004. The Associated Press would later vote it as Colorado's top 2004 news story.

On Jan. 27, 2004, the CU football team suddenly became more famous than the team that had won the national championship 15 years earlier and, just as suddenly, seemed to have gone to the top of the list of out-of-control college football programs.

CU's leap to the media center stage was at first hard to figure. After all, it had been more than a year since co-ed Lisa Simpson had filed a lawsuit claiming she was raped at a December 2001 party held at her home and attended by several Colorado football players and recruits. It had been almost a year since four players pleaded guilty to contributing to the delinquency of minors for bringing alcohol or marijuana to that party.

A year had gone by since CU coach Gary Barnett had revoked the scholarships of four players who attended the party.

As part of my job covering the federal courts in Denver, I had written about the case several times since it was filed in December of 2002. I also attended all of the early hearings in the case. I had never had a problem getting a front-row seat in the new-smelling courtroom at the sparkling new Alfred J. Arraj Federal Courthouse. Reporters from both the giant Denver dailies and even the *Boulder Daily Camera*, a newspaper located a few blocks from CU's athletic complex in Boulder, had paid virtually no attention to the case. The case of CU co-ed Anne Gilmore, who filed a nearly identical suit only months after Simpson, had also been largely ignored. All of that changed on January 27, 2004.

Satellite trucks the likes of which had not been seen since the trial of Oklahoma City bomber Timothy McVeigh lined the downtown streets outside the Denver federal courthouse that day. Inside the ninth-floor courtroom 15-20 reporters milled around waiting for a routine hearing to start.

Why were they all there, I wondered. Was someone giving away free hair spray?

Some of these reporters need directions to even get to the federal courthouse, I thought. Why did they come on this day?

The hearing itself that day was rather routine. U.S. Magistrate Craig Schaffer ruled in favor of a motion compelling Simpson to submit to a psychiatric exam and ordered her to turn over more portions of her diary during the discovery process. After hotly-contested arguments from both sides, he ruled that since Simpson was claiming emotional suffering and was planning to introduce evidence from her own psychiatrist, CU's lawyers had the right to have her examined by a psychiatrist of their choosing. Instead of allowing the sides to endlessly argue over what portions of the diary would be turned over, Schaffer ordered the diary turned over to him. He would then decide which portions were relevant to the case.

Pretty standard stuff. I assumed that would be story in the next morning's papers.

During a break in the hearing, however, I was approached by a blond woman in a black suit. What followed was anything but standard stuff.

"I'm Lisa Simon of Prescient Communications," she said. "I represent Lisa Simpson. If you would like a copy of (District Attorney) Mary Keenan's deposition, they can be picked up tomorrow at her lawyer's office. Here's my card."

She was certainly the most cooperative press agent I'd met in a while. She was also the first press agent I'd ever seen in a civil case. For some reason, I didn't find it strange that a college sophomore from a working-class family had a publicist. Neither did anyone else in the media. We should have.

Simon, who had previously worked as a press agent for the family of Dylan Klebold, one of the killers in the horrific Columbine High School massacre about 10 miles from the federal courthouse, was, in my opinion, now calling the tune in a story that would destroy careers, lives and reputations. She, as she would admit to me days later, was setting the agenda—one I soon suspected was designed to bring down the CU football program without regard for the merits of a lawsuit that, upon further inspection, was more dubious than any of us had reported.

That's what all those TV reporters were doing there.

I began to think that Lisa Simon had invited at least some of them. Their editors hadn't been sending them to any of the CU hearings.

After a few days of my self-imposed lockdown, I called Barnett and asked him if he had ever seen that Sally Field movie, "Absence of Malice."

"Yes," he said.

"Remember how Sally Field wrote a story that wasn't true, but had been planted for her to bite on?" I asked. "We just fell for the same thing. We are all Sally Field."

"Yes, you are," he said.

He wasn't laughing.

By now, neither was I.

I was mad—at myself and at the rest of the reporters who had allowed political correctness to hijack factual correctness, not to mention fairness and balance.

I would soon come to believe that that sexism—and probably racism—had also hijacked feminism in Boulder.

In the weeks following that January hearing, horrifying accusations against CU piled up like defenders on a loose football. At first, three women claimed to have been raped either at or after the infamous party. Then the number grew to six. Then it grew to nine and eventually to 10. Advocates tossed out accusations that named neither the victim nor the perpetrator. In mid-February, Barnett would be suspended for three months for his comments about the kicking skills of former kicker Katie Hnida, who claimed to have been raped by a teammate.

It was as though the allegations had been stockpiled, organized, carefully orchestrated and peeled off like the layers of an onion during the February ratings period. To me it seemed a little too coincidental.

Meanwhile, the media seemed unwilling to investigate both sides of the story in a political climate under which all allegations of sexual misconduct are considered to be true and under which anyone who questions an allegation is a "victim basher "—even in the absence of evidence and criminal charges.

During my 11-day self-imposed exile, I collected boxes of documents, police reports, depositions and witness statements. While I was living on potato chips, coffee and cigarettes, the light started to come on. It was Lisa Simon, the press agent for the accusers, who accidentally threw the switch on that light. I had seen a statement by Barnett on Fox Sports Rocky Mountain's 10 p.m. sportscast and decided to call her for a comment.

"I'm not going to comment on that," she said. "We have our agenda and we're sticking with it."

She shouldn't have told me that. The word "agenda" hit me like ton of bricks. Damn, I thought. They must have planned this whole thing. They knew what they were going to release and not release and when. Their plan was a stroke of public-relations genius and it appeared to me that they were now in control of every newsroom in the state. The national media would soon join their band of lackeys. Figuring out what happened was only half the chore. The other half, writing about what I had found, was more difficult. And scary. I gave some thought to abandoning the project and just falling in step with the rest of them, but decided I couldn't do that. There was big news here that people who buy newspapers hadn't been allowed to see. That news largely involved the media itself. I would have to convince my own editors to run the story and would also have to face the consequences of airing the media's dirty laundry.

If I'm not right, I'm finished in this business, I thought. If I am right, I might still be finished, I worried.

But I became convinced I was right.

I had to write the story.

In addition to the public documents that anyone could have purchased for 15 cents a page, I uncovered an even more explosive document – the first volume of Lisa Simpson's deposition in the case. That document had been sealed under a federal court order since the end of January—coincidentally the same time Simpson's press agent had released Boulder District Attorney Mary Keenan's deposition. Simpson's lawyers were on one hand sealing documents that didn't flatter their client, while on the other hand distributing documents that served as unflattering press releases for CU. It looked to me as though they didn't want the public to see Simpson's unfiltered deposition and certainly weren't going to encourage reporters to examine the statements and police reports that cast doubt on their claims or placed the story in a different light.

My editors at the *Longmont Daily Times-Call*, a daily newspaper located about 30 miles from Denver and about 10 miles from Boulder, approved the story in advance but put me on a short leash. Since I covered the Denver area and specifically the federal courts, I worked from my house in south Denver and rarely went to Boulder County. As the story developed, time was critical. It was already too late to undo the unfairness that had victimized CU, I thought. Every day that went by made it even more so, if that's possible. As work on the story progressed, it was decided that it would run on Friday, Feb. 27. Most of our big stories ran on Sundays, but I didn't want to wait until then. We owed it to our readers, as well as to fairness and decency, to run it as soon as possible. I wanted the story on the street fast.

While conducting interviews for that story, I got a hint of the ramifications it was going to cerate. I called Boulder District Attorney Mary Keenan for comment on her role in the civil suit and at first the conversation was routine and civil.

Keenan freely admitted that, after failing to uncover enough evidence to charge any players with sexual assault, she charged four of them with felony contribution to the delinquency of minors in order to squeeze some sort of justice from the case. She said that while the evidence didn't support rape charges, she believed Simpson's claim and filed the charges "to get accountability." She further claimed that she often files lesser charges in cases where she can't prove a more serious offense. Keenan said she advised Simpson of her legal right to sue in civil court because she is required to do so under Colorado law and said she gave Simpson "a list of three-to-five lawyers" who specialized in those types of cases. Saying she had never met the people who later became Simpson's lawyers before Simpson hired them, she certainly became close with them once they were on board.

The DA also admitted she met with Simpson's lawyers over lunch just before Christmas in 2003, a year after the suit was filed. During that meeting, she said, the Simpson team "pointed out potential criminal charges stemming from the depositions." Keenan said the Simpson team, which was "ethically bound" to report crimes arising from civil litigation, was seeking charges of perjury and evidence tampering. Pretty serious stuff. It would later be revealed that among the targets of Simpson's lawyers was Gary Barnett, who they alleged had lied in a deposition. Now they were doing their civic duty by notifying the DA of potential criminal conduct stemming from a civil case. Keenan then got sarcastic about the lunch meeting.

"I paid for my own lunch," she said. "I can't remember what I ordered."

Keenan also admitted meeting for about an hour with a Simpson attorney on the morning of her deposition in October of 2003. She said during that meeting she was also provided with a copy of a newspaper article in which she had been quoted in order to "refresh her memory" about what she had said in the article. She saw nothing unusual or unethical about any of her dealings, but her relationship with Simpson's counsel was starting to look a little cozy to me. Keenan said she met with Chris Ford, one of Simpson's attorneys, "two or three times" before the suit was filed and even received portions of a draft of the suit, which was filed in December of 2002. She claimed, "I wasn't sent the whole complaint" and only received the portions that involved her. The portion that involved her, of course, would become the cornerstone of Simpson press agent Lisa Simon's publicity campaign. Although she didn't bring it up, she had received at least one other piece of the case, a document produced a year after the suit was filed and one that was highly critical of Keenan. Less than two weeks before her explosive deposition was released, she contacted at least one newspaper and provided it with a copy—complete with her on-the-record rebuttal of its contents.

That document, which became known as the "Early Report," was commissioned by CU's defense lawyers and was written by Norm Early, a former Denver District Attorney. The report, based on an examination of thousands of documents generated in the police investigation of the rape, blasted Keenan's handling of the case and, even more to maddening to Keenan, criticized the fact that the four people charged in the case were black men. The report also questioned why none of the white females who admitted breaking the law was charged. Early also blasted Keenan for publicly maintaining that the rapes took place, even after she declined to file charges because of what she called "identity issues" in the case. CU wide receiver Ron Monteilh knew a little about identity problems in the case. He was initially charged, but the charge was dismissed because he was mistakenly identified in a photo lineup. That identification was the only evidence against Montielh.

While the Early Report wasn't in the case file and was only available to the lawyers in the case, Keenan had somehow gotten a copy. Only the plaintiff's lawyers and CU's lawyers had access to it and CU's lawyers probably wouldn't have given the report to a trial witness who would be adverse to them. That narrowed it down considerably. Her relationship to the Simpson legal team was obviously closer than she had admitted. They were the most likely source of the report, which couldn't have made her any madder. About nine days before her deposition became public, she called Travis Henry, the assistant city editor of the Longmont paper and a former reporter who has covered her office. According to Henry, Keenan asked him to come to Boulder to meet with her and said she had something for him. At that meeting, Keenan gave Henry a copy of the Early Report and said she wanted to comment on it.

On the record.

In her remarks to Henry, Keenan got personal in her attack on Early. "I know more in one finger about sexual assault than

Norm Early knows in his whole body," she said. She also told Henry she was leaking the report because of the "beating" she had been taking on the sports talk shows. What beating was that, I thought when I heard that comment? I followed the CU situation on all those shows, and hadn't heard a word about the Early Report. When Henry learned that I was exploring the Keenan angle for my story, he called me and told me he had something for me that he had gotten a week ago. It was the Early Report. When I saw it, the depth of Keenan's role in the Simpson civil case started to become clearer. Apparently Keenan never imagined that anyone would ask her where she got the report. She was right. No reporter ever did. I told my editors that it looked as though Keenan had one foot in the criminal case and the other foot in the civil case.

My interview with Keenan, meanwhile, turned into a cross-examination by the district attorney herself.

"Why are you asking these questions?"

"What is this story going to say?"

"Is it going to make me look bad?"

She sure had a lot of questions. Finally I had to tell her, "Mary, I'm the one asking the questions here." She left me with an ominous warning. "If this story makes me look bad, I'm going to be pissed off," she said. "And I'm mean when I'm pissed off."

Ron Monteilh probably wouldn't disagree with that. I was getting a little pissed myself, but decided not to get into a shouting match with her. I didn't need her going over my head — a worry I considered to be legitimate given my past experience with her predecessor, Alex Hunter, and many other Boulder County politicians.

Another part of Keenan's conversation with Henry also served to indicate her knowledge of the case was greater than she had admitted. She told Henry other depositions in the case, including that of former assistant athletic director Bob

Chichester, would bolster her assertion that CU ignored warnings given by her in 1998. How did she know that? Copies of Chichester's deposition, which weren't in the court file, wouldn't be leaked to anyone in the media for weeks and she had obviously already read it. Simpson's lawyers, the only ones with access to the report outside CU, seemed to be keeping the DA updated on their case.

When my article was published, it created little stir in the local media. Five weeks later it would create a federal court hearing. While we e-mailed copies of the story around the country in hopes of national attention I naively thought would turn the course of the media coverage, that national attention didn't materialize.

Other reporters ignored the press agent and the DA's role in the suit. Jim Hughes, a federal court beat reporter for the *Denver Post*, told me "that stuff in your story is wrong."

"What stuff?" I asked.

"The stuff about Channel 9 getting the Keenan deposition. I'm in a position to know. My paper has a partnership with Channel 9." He was actually bragging about his paper's alliance with a TV station that "shares" stories a day after it runs them. Nice partner, I thought.

The part of my story that created a storm involved Lisa Simpson's deposition, which had been put under seal by the court at the end of January. In that deposition, lawyers for CU quoted excerpts from her diary in which she said, "God help me, I will ruin the lives of Joseph Allen Mackey, Marques Harris, Corey Alexander, Ron Monteilh, Jesse Wallace and whoever the recruits are." She went on to say she believed that while she couldn't identify any of her alleged attackers, she was glad they were in trouble and that "they should have been punished because they contributed to minors anyway." She then admitted that she, too, had given alcohol to minors. At first Simpson's lead attorney, Baine Kerr, was the only one who confronted me on the document he thought was sealed.

"You are in violation of two federal court orders," he roared over the phone at me.

"No I'm not. I'm not under that court order. You are," I responded. "You know better than that."

Kerr was every bit as pissed as Keenan had promised to be. He complained about me referring to Lisa Simon as being from Prescient Communications. "You made it sound like a big agency," he said. "Lisa Simon basically IS Prescient Communications." So what? I thought. For being a small company, she sure did a big job. Kerr also ordered me to not call Simon again for anything.

Except for Kerr's outburst, the story rotted for about five weeks. Then one morning I ran into Rick Sallinger, a reporter for Denver CBS affiliate Channel 4, at the federal courthouse. Sallinger, who is probably the best TV reporter in Denver and who does a thorough job on his stories, asked me if he could have copy of the Simpson deposition. He had recently done a story that featured an edited version of the video tape of that deposition. His station had gotten it through the Colorado Open Records Act the day before Simpson's lawyers filed a motion to seal it. At the time of the request, CU had no choice but to give them a copy. It was a public record at that point. When it was subsequently sealed, both CU and Simpson's lawyers asked Channel 4 to give it back—after broadcasting it. Channel 4 refused, and I admired Sallinger for being the only TV reporter in town to think of requesting the tape instead of just waiting for spoon-fed leaks from the Simpson team like everyone else.

I wanted to give the deposition to Rick, but figured it might get me in trouble at work. I finally told him, "I'll bring it to you when I come back here this afternoon." I thought, what the heck. I used it five weeks ago. It's just gathering dust at my house and this story needs to get out. While at the copying machine at the courthouse with Rick later that afternoon, I ran into Lyn Bartels from Denver's other big daily newspaper, the *Rocky Mountain News*. Lyn, one of that paper's best reporters, naturally wanted her own copy. I gave it to her. Channel 4 did a story that night and the *Rocky Mountain News* carried a story the next morning. Simpson's lawyers, according to the reporters, called both offices and told them they had better stop violating the court order that had sealed the document. A few hours after Lyn's story appeared, Jim Hughes from the *Denver Post* called me. He wanted a copy. The same guy who the previous month thought I was an idiot now needed a favor. But I wanted the story to get wider play, even if it meant helping a newspaper and a reporter for which I had no respect.

"I'm not sure what or if we're going to do with it," he said.

"I don't care what you do with it. The *Rocky* already beat you. You can have it," I told him. I later found out he had been called on the carpet for getting beaten on yet another CU-related story.

After calling my editors and reportedly brow-beating the *Post*, the *Rocky* and Channel 4, Simpson's attorneys decided to take legal action. They filed a motion for sanctions against CU on the assumption that CU's lawyers leaked the Simpson deposition to the *Post*, the *Rocky* and Channel 4. Interestingly enough, they took no such action when the Keenan and Chichester depositions found their way to the public. During a subsequent hearing, Kerr stood up and demanded sanctions, and CU's lawyers just let him talk. Finally, CU attorney David Temple told U.S. Magistrate Craig Schaffer that I had given them the document and had told him so that morning in a phone call. That was true.

"We're in a bit of a bind here," Temple had told me when he called earlier in the day. "You don't have to answer this, but did you give that deposition to those guys?"

"Yes, I did," I said. "Tell them I admitted it." I figured I couldn't get in any more trouble than what I was already in. Bartels and I both stayed away from the hearing. I didn't want Simpson's lawyers to pick me out of the crowd and demand that I take the stand. I had no intention of telling the magistrate or anyone else where I got the Simpson deposition.

The magistrate denied the sanctions and the deposition story looked like it would die. But it didn't. On April 29, media columnist Michael Roberts, who writes for the Denver alternative weekly *Westword*, wrote a column about the leaked Simpson deposition. Roberts had called me for comments the week before the piece came out, so I knew the column would create more bad blood. I had given him what he called "great quotes," which in our business meant inflammatory quotes. When Roberts told me that Lisa Simon had insisted that she wasn't soliciting the media at that Jan. 27 hearing that resulted in the leaking of the Keenan deposition, I got mad. According to Simon, she was only there to put media faces with names.

"It was like she was standing on the street corner going 'Hi, sailor,'" I told him. "It's campaigning, it's politicking, it's advertising, it's trying the case in the newspapers. She can call it anything she wants, but I was there. I saw it."

Roberts printed nearly every word I said. He also printed the part where I compared the Denver media to Sally Field's character in "Absence of Malice," who ran with planted- but-inaccurate information that made the public believe that Paul Newman's character was under investigation for a murder. "We were all Sally Field for a while." I told him. "It's just that some of us pulled our heads out and figured out that we were getting used. Most of us did not." I was getting angrier by the minute and went on to refer to Channel 9 reporter Adam Schrager, who led the sweeps-month assault with the first copy of the Keenan deposition, as "Sally Schrager." Roberts printed that, too. I figured my bosses would have a stroke when they read the *Westword* article, but they never mentioned it.

Schrager, however, was really mad and sent an e-mail to Roberts threatening to come up with a nickname for Roberts that would stick with him. After obtaining my home e-mail from a now-former friend of mine who also worked at Channel 9, he also sent me three e-mails saying I had wronged him. At one point he said I owed it to him to sit down and talk about things. "You at least owe me a drink," he said. Why, I thought? I don't drink.

While my editors said nothing about my comments to *Westword*, they got really unhappy about my sharing of the deposition with the other outlets. I was "written up" for giving the Simpson depositions to other media outlets and violating some company policy by not getting their permission. I had to sign some piece of paper acknowledging that I had been disciplined. I signed it, but told them I would do the same thing again under the same circumstances. I wondered out loud why we had a policy that kept me from giving out information we used five weeks ago. We are in the business of informing people, I thought. Ironically, my editors purposely didn't want to know anything while I was researching the story and uncovering sealed documents that helped sell their newspaper. To me it seemed like they had put me out to sea in a cardboard boat and then second-guessed my decision to get our story, an important but ignored one, out to the public.

During the remainder of 2004, I continued digging into every available piece of information regarding the allegations. I watched as CU linebacker Akarika Dawn hired a lawyer and held a press conference after he was wrongly identified as one of "two large black men" suspected of drugging and raping a woman they had met at a Boulder bar. The source of those allegations was a bartender who told police that since the two men were big and black, he assumed they were football players. Subsequent DNA tests would prove that neither Dawn nor the other un-named player could have assaulted the woman. Before that exoneration, however, both the newspapers and TV stations—based on a leak from the Boulder Police Department—reported that two football players were under investigation for the woman's rape. When the two were cleared, the print got much smaller.

To me, it looked like the CU story was turning into an old-fashioned lynching.

While both the veracity and motives of those referred to by CU players as "The Haters" appeared to crumble under the light of basic journalistic scrutiny, there was no such scrutiny among the media.

Headlines, not evidence, were creating guilt—a guilt that would subject 100 young football players, many of them black, to obscene catcalls from opposing fans, racially hateful e-mails directed at players dating white women and the wrath of a media afraid to be labeled as victim bashers.

Former rape counselor Megan Rogers, who had displayed a level of ethics and guts not yet shown by any reporter covering the case, was one who found herself carrying the label of victim basher. She was dismissed from her part-time job after showing her superiors a study that discredited an earlier report the organization was using in its training and literature. Rogers, who was told the discredited report would continue to be used because the cause was more important than the truth, would later have her say before the committee that investigated the allegations. Her story, however, didn't draw the same media interest as the broad-brush allegations offered by other activists.

By the spring of 2004 I had a lot of questions.

Who are these 100 young men whose lives and personalities are hidden under helmets and pads? Who are their parents? What do they do when they aren't playing football? How would they react to being labeled as the worse thugs in college football?

Could they live with a criminal probe of the 2001 party that resulted in the felony indictment of four black players but no charges against the white women who admitted to the same offenses and no charges against the white man who admitted supplying a case of Keystone beer? Would anyone listen to their side of the story, driven by what to me looked like race, gender, hate and politics?

I decided to find answers to those questions. I wanted to see for myself what kind of program Barnett was running and what kind of people were in that program. Surprisingly, it took only one phone call to Barnett to get the access I needed. He quickly agreed to let me inside the football team for the entire season. I figured I would have to negotiate long and hard with him, but that wasn't the case.

"You're in," he said. That was it.

During the 2004 season I virtually lived with the Colorado football team. I was given access to practices, meetings, film sessions, meals, chapel services, the locker room and sidelines and even the bus rides to unfriendly stadiums around the country.

Some of the sports beat writers weren't too thrilled about my new-found access. During a road trip to Seattle in the second week of the season I had lunch with our beat writer, Steve Hemphill, and B.G. Brooks, the CU beat writer from the *Rocky Mountain News*. Brooks was friendly to me at lunch, but later that afternoon went to CU sports information director David Plati to complain about my access to the team. He was concerned that I was getting interviews with players after they were in their rooms on the nights before games. That, of course, wasn't the case. I had no intention of bothering them in their rooms and have no idea where Brooks got that idea. The beat writers kept much closer track of things like who was injured and who was going to play than I did. They didn't get it. I wasn't writing about football. I was writing about people. After that Seattle trip I tried to avoid the press box whenever possible. I didn't trust those guys, including Brooks, whom I had known and liked for years. Later in the year I would find that my distrust was well placed.

From Labor Day through Thanksgiving, I traveled, ate, laughed and cried with the players. I sweated and froze on their sideline and walked what seemed a thousand miles in the shoes of young men who weren't at the party and who weren't accused of crimes, but who still carried the stigma of broad-brush allegations that would haunt them the rest of their lives.

During that same time I documented the conduct of a district attorney whose criminal filing decisions in the CU case appeared to me to be driven at least in part by race and gender issues and whose political history had included attempts to stifle media coverage of legal problems involving one of her employees and her two grown children. Reporters who covered Keenan's office for years would document those tales of manipulation and bullying.

I documented the conduct of Colorado Governor Bill Owens, who, armed only with Keenan's self-serving deposition, called the CU football team "an embarrassment to the state," while apparently trying to divert attention from his own personal failings after separating from his wife because of his alleged infidelity. It was Owens who, in spite of having almost no knowledge of the situation, told CU officials to reel in their runaway football program "Or I will." I also examined the role of CU Regent Cindy Carlisle, who presented herself as a reformer while pushing aside questions about the conflict of interest created by her marriage to the lead attorney in the civil suits, and the conduct of fellow regent Jim Martin, who got lots of TV face time in his failed attempt to initiate a house-cleaning in the athletic department and by calling on the NCAA to institute recruiting reforms that it had actually initiated weeks before he spoke. At a press conference outside the Denver Civic Center, Martin drooped out of the race for another term as a regent and issued his challenge to the NCAA while a group of bored reporters took notes. Behind the reporters stood a small group of winos who had stopped to hear some guy give a speech. Some of the winos cheered as Martin's voice rose in righteous indignation. I'm sure none of them knew who he was or what he was talking about. It was the funniest thing I saw during the nightmare of the CU recruiting scandal.

My investigation of the veracity and motivations of the accusers themselves resulted in revelations of inconsistent stories, vows of vengeance against men regardless of guilt or innocence and manipulation by politicians, lawyers and their own press agent.

Most disturbingly, the investigation exposed a media that to this day is unwilling to admit its own mistakes and even more unwilling to correct them. What began as a major media-fueled scandal eventually sputtered to a halt in the absence of substance or truth and adversely affected many innocent people.

During the first week of the 2004 season I watched as the CU football team was able to at least temporarily force the replacement of scandal stories with football stories. During the second week I would travel to Seattle for the team's first road trip of the season and its first taste of already-hostile crowds made more hostile by the scandal allegations.

Chapter Four
Up in Here

When the CU football team visited Seattle for its second game of the season, it shouldn't have felt much like a road trip. Boulder and Seattle had a lot in common.

While Seattle is a lot larger and has much more water than land-locked Boulder, the cities have much in common. Both feature a high-tech industry employing an educated, upscale workforce, many of whom spend their lunch hours running in the rain or sweating at the gym. Purveyors of bicycle helmets and running shoes in either town are not likely to miss any meals.

As residents of Boulder, the members of the CU football team were used to seeing affluence and affluent white people all around them. The players, however, saw little of the Emerald City during their trip to play Washington State. Fresh off a last-second win over in-state rival Colorado State in their first game, the Buffs went straight from the Seattle airport to Qwest Field, normally the home of the NFL Seattle Seahawks, but this week the site of Washington State's annual "home" game 300 miles away from its home in Pullman.

The Buffs were making a rare trip to Seattle, the city that Boeing, Microsoft and Starbucks built, a city that is a handful of coffee shops away from displacing New York as the City that Never Sleeps.

After a 90-minute walk-through practice, the buses took the team to suburban Bellevue, an upscale community not unlike Boulder. German cars idled at stoplights outside the Bellevue Hyatt that served as headquarters for the team and party central for the CU fans who made the trip. By the time the team arrived from its practice late Friday afternoon, the drinks were flowing in the Hyatt. Black and gold balloons hung in the lobby and fans wrapped Heineken bottles in drink-coolers shaped like CU football jerseys.

There was no such atmosphere among the players. After their Friday night meal—the same prime rib, chicken and lasagna menu they devoured on the eve of games both at home and on the road—the players were allowed to visit with friends and family in the lobby. At 9:30 p.m. the players took advantage of a snack table, piling plates with pizza and sandwiches for the trip back to their rooms before the 10:45 lights-out.

"No visitors except on the first floor," Barnett repeated to his team before the trip. "No do-rags on the bus."

Hotel visitors tried to look inconspicuous as they eyed the group of large black men dressed in black sweat suits. The players, however, should have been used to standing out. At CU, a school where only 394 of the Boulder campus's 24,710 students were black, race was apparent. Black students made up only 1.6 percent of the student population, according to a 1999 study conducted by the university's own Office of Diversity and Equality. That report also called the school's black population "under-represented when compared to the state's (4 percent black) population."

More than 40 percent of the players on CU's numerical roster for 2004 were black. The team depth chart, which indicates which players get playing time, carried a higher percentage. Even my crude mathematics skills told me the football team accounted for nearly 10 percent of CU-Boulder's black student population. Those numbers made for a sense of solidarity among the players.

Of the many problems the team faced in the wake of the scandal, racial unity, the players said, was not among them.

"There is no race in our locker room," tackle Matt McChesney said. "The only colors are black and gold."

Wide receiver Ron Monteilh, who was wrongfully accused of contributing to the delinquency of a minor in connection with

"The Party" three years earlier, said, "Some of the coolest guys on the team are white." Monteilh, who graduated from lily-white Beverly Hills High School, was used to being one of the few blacks on a team. The fifth-year senior, whose family moved to the outer edge of the 90210 ZIP code when he was in the ninth grade, said he spent "nearly every weekend" with white teammates such as McChesney and tackle Sam Wilder, a white Texan. "When I was at Oregon State (for one year) most of the players hung out with guys of their own race. It's not like that here," he said. Racial unity among the players, however, didn't mean there was an abundance of tolerance on the rest of the campus. During the winter of 2004 members of the team reported receiving hate-filled e-mails attacking interracial dating between black men and white women. During the 2004-2005 school year a black student reportedly struck a white student who had called him a "nigger" and both were charged in the incident. In the spring of 2005 CU player Stephone Robinson received two racially-threatening e-mails while living in the supposedly-liberal bastion of Boulder.

Unlike many schools in the Big 12 Conference, which has several teams in former slave states, CU has had black players for 50 years. One of those, offensive lineman John Wooten, became only the third black player at the school when he enrolled in the fall of 1955, a time when conferences in the West and Midwest were offering opportunities that wouldn't come to black athletes in the South for two decades. Wooten, who is often called the best lineman CU ever produced, excelled at CU and in the NFL and had a long career as an NFL front-office executive. He says he was just glad to get a scholarship and didn't give any thought to playing in a nearly all-white town.

"That never really entered my mind," he said. "I looked at it as an opportunity to get an education and play at a big school. Back then black players couldn't get served at restaurants at places like Kansas State and when we played in the Orange Bowl in Florida."

But, Florida, Kansas and the rest of the country have come a long way since black athletes had to travel to the hinterlands to find opportunities to play and had to eat and sometimes stay at different places than their white teammates. The racial barriers that kept southern football teams all-white began to crumble a decade after Wooten entered CU. Ahead of that curve was Texas Western College, which integrated its football team in 1955, nine years before the passage of the landmark Civil Rights Act of 1964. Texas Western, which is now known as the University of Texas–El Paso, would make history 10 years later when its predominantly–black basketball team defeated the legendary Adolph Rupp's all-white University of Kentucky team for the national championship.

The University of Florida integrated its athletic teams in 1968 on the orders of university president Stephen C. O'Connell, who saw the school's segregated teams as a violation of the Civil Rights Act of 1964, which guaranteed equal access to people of all races. In Alabama, where Governor George Wallace had stood in a University of Alabama doorway to block integration, change came slowly. The 'Bama football team was all-white until 1970, when the Crimson tide was manhandled 42-21 by the University of Southern California in what was then considered the national championship game. USC was led by two black running backs, Sam Cunningham and Clarence Davis, who would later find great success in the National Football League. It seems the embarrassment of losing, not civil rights legislation, spurred integration at Alabama.

According to a December 2004 article on NBCSports.com, there are currently around 10,000 scholarship players at the nation's 117 Division One football schools. Half of those, according to the article, are black. However, opportunities for black head coaches have not kept pace with the integration seen on Saturday afternoons. Prior to the 2004 season, Sylvester Croom was hired as the first-ever black coach at Mississippi State University and became only the fifth member of the Division One black coaching fraternity. That number would drop to only two at the end of the 2004 season when Tony Samuel was fired by New Mexico State University, Tyrone Willingham was fired by Notre Dame and Fitz Hill resigned from his job at San Jose State University. The number of black head coaches at Division One schools would later jump back to three when Willingham was hired by the University of Washington. Those three coaches now represent just over 2 percent of the nation's Division One head coaches at a time when over half the players are African American.

While most Americans take the integration of college football for granted, some are still fighting it. The American Nationalist Union, a group that claims to fight for the rights of what it calls America's forgotten majority but which preaches only thinly-veiled racism, has a section on its Web site dedicated to "Caste Football." That section decries the absence of white athletes on both the college and professional levels and even has its own All-America football team. "Here are the best white football players in the country," writer J.B. Cash said in announcing the organization's 2004 team. The ANU Web site also features articles with headlines such as "1-A Football Programs Refuse to Recruit Star White Running Backs" and one article laments facts such as, "There are no white starting cornerbacks in the NFL out of 64 players who start at that position," and "There are no starting white tailbacks." The ANU Web site also features an article about University of Mississippi supporter Edward "Red" Graham, who is on a mission to "de-integrate" the Ole Miss football program. Graham, who, according to the article insists that black visitors to his home come in the back door, said, "I refuse to attend any football games which are integrated." He has also undertaken a campaign to get Croom fired from his job at Mississippi State. The article doesn't say how many blacks have visited Graham's home, but that same racial intolerance we expect to see only in the Old Deep South has officially reared its head in Boulder in the past two years.

While most of the country would gag on the ANU's racist drivel, even so-called liberal communities like Boulder can seem like the Old South to black athletes who have grown up in predominantly-black neighborhoods or cities.

And for good reason.

Cornerback Mike Spivey came to Boulder in 1973, nearly 20 years after John Wooten, but was hit with culture shock even before he attended his first class. "My first day on campus I saw a squirrel in a tree and started throwing rocks at it," he said. "A guy came up to me and said, 'We don't do that around here.' I said some pretty ugly things to him—I made him feel very uncomfortable. He was right. You shouldn't throw rocks at squirrels, but where I came from it was all right. It was a big cultural difference. I got that lesson on my first day, before I even attended a class. I was in a different place with different rules."

Spivey was raised in Houston, where he became a football star at all-black George Washington Carver High School. "We didn't have any white students," he said. "The only white people were teachers. Boulder was a very different place."

Spivey's rock-throwing confrontation was only the beginning of the lessons he would learn as a black athlete recruited to play football in a nearly-all white town. Although he was an honor student at de facto-segregated Carver High in Houston, he struggled early and often at CU. Language was a problem right off the bat. "You're taught English in Texas, but it's a different dialect," he said. "I turned in my first English paper and got a 'D' on it." It didn't take him long to realize the differences between

American English and Southern English, especially black dialect. While most white people long ago came to realize that the term "bad" can be used to mean very good, many white people are still left wondering when they hear the terms "finna or "finta," both of which shortened versions of the southern expression "fixing to." They don't understand that the word "here" is often replaced with the phrase "up in here." They are also baffled when young black men call each other "nigger" or "nigga." Although the term is used as an informal term of solidarity among young black men, some older blacks cringe at its use. Spivey is one of them. "These young brothers weren't around when that term was used by a lot of whites," he said. "They have no idea of the hate that went with that word."

CU's black players got a taste of what that word meant during 2004 when most received those hate-filed e-mails aimed at interracial dating, a practice that goes on at every campus in the country but is rarely mentioned. The media, in fact, never mentioned that the four players charged in the wake of the December 7, 2001 party that shook the foundation of the CU football program were black. While reporters may argue that race is no longer important in news stories in this enlightened age, it was an issue in the CU story. The reporters hid behind their own race-is-unimportant-anymore creed as they ignored the obvious racial overtones of the entire "scandal."

While the media has been asleep at the wheel, those overtones have been discussed privately in Boulder for years. Ask any black male athlete what the term "DWB" stands for in Boulder and he will quickly provide the answer. It's the same answer Mike Spivey learned 30 years ago. "Driving While Black," he said, "but it goes beyond that. When you walk into a store, ride a bike, you are looked at differently. Athletes have been stopped for not having a light on their bike at night. The hardest part is that it's insulting because the rest of the population is not being targeted." Spivey also pointed out CU's school policy banning "aggressive language," a ban he believes is racially-motivated and associated with former running back Eric Bienemy's widely-publicized confrontation with a white female parking lot guard years after he left the school, a confrontation that resulted in his ban from campus. Barnett would later take heat for hiring Bienemy as the team's running-backs coach.

In the complaint accompanying Lisa Simpson's civil suit, her lawyer would cite Bienemy's employment as an example of a lawless football program. That same suit also cited the 2003 shooting of basketball player Chris Copeland, who was the random victim of a drive-by shooting at a party he was attending. An investigation determined that Copeland was not the target of the random shooting. His wounds were not life threatening, but he still has a bullet buried in his body. And he is black. It's hard for me to imagine what the story of a black basketball player being randomly shot has to do with a suit claiming the football team was out of control and responsible for rapes.

Spivey said it took him about two years to "get used to" life as a black athlete in an affluent white community. "You had to learn that you were treated differently during different times of the year," he said. "You were treated much better during the football season. At other times you were expendable, even to the coaches." Spivey, who avoided the pitfalls of drugs and alcohol that tormented his generation but who admits to having been "very violent" as a young man, became the CU football team chaplain six years ago in part because "I wish someone had had been there to explain things to me when I was that age." Spivey said the chip he carried on his shoulder as a young man made his life difficult and "shortened my NFL career." A man who once "sought out violence and found ways to start it," Spivey has since experienced a religious transformation and now ministers to troubled-youth groups and prisoners in addition to his traveling-chaplain role with the CU football team. A staunch defender of the CU players, Spivey said their initial reaction to the rape allegations was confusion. "Initially, they were bombarded with so much negative information, they wondered themselves about their innocence or guilt. Our system is good at negative programming or providing a lot of negative information and the public believes that information." Spivey said the players were also hamstrung by what he believes was the university's virtual prohibition against anyone defending themselves. "The whole nation was affected by it," he said. "In every stadium they were all convicted. What forum did they have to defend themselves? They had none."

In September they would look for that forum on the football field.

But they probably weren't thinking about race as the buses took them across Puget Sound through neighborhoods where former CU coach Rick Neuheisel's $5 million home was not even the biggest house on the block. Players gazed out at homes with boat ramps for back yards as they anticipated the greeting they would receive in their first trip outside Boulder since the scandal broke.

The Buffs heard only a handful of fans screaming "rapists" as they jogged on the field for pre-game warm-ups. There were no protesters holding "No Means No" signs. Those would come later. Much like they would all year, the players ignored the taunts. The 67,000-seat stadium was not quite full, but tensions not related to the sex scandal rose between the teams as the game approached. Just before retreating to the locker room after warm-ups, the CU players gathered and danced up and down on a circle at midfield, right on top of the Washington State logo. The

Cougars weren't happy with that display and the referees stepped in to separate the two squads. Barnett would later order his team to cease dancing on other teams' logos, but the pre-game display was not ignored in the locker room just before the game started.

"All ya'll went and started some shit up in here," one of the CU players yelled out as the team got ready to take the field minutes later. "We better be ready to back it up."

As the team ran out on the field, ABC-TV's game announcers, like those at Fox Sports the week before, mentioned CU's notoriety off the field. As play-by-play announcer Gary Thorne set the lineups, color announcer Ed Cunningham mentioned the team's "tumultuous off season." The game, which had originally been scheduled to be played on September 15, 2001, had been cancelled because of the September 11 terrorist attacks. Three seasons later it was about to kick off on September 11, exactly three years since the attacks. Just before the kickoff, sideline reporter Suzy Shuster asked Barnett if he thought his team was emotionally shot after last week's last-second win over Colorado State, saying she thought the Buffs "might be drained this week."

"I'm not concerned," Barnett told her. "We play with passion, not emotion. I don't think we drained ourselves. I think that's the way this team plays all year." When asked what changes the coaching staff had made in the secondary in the wake of being torched for 403 yards the week before, Barnett didn't budge. Besides looking for way to get to the quarterback more often, there had been no changes. "We'll, we've just gotten better," he said.

At least the defense had. The offense managed only a field goal in the first half, which ended in a 3-3 tie. At halftime Barnett told his team they were letting emotion override passion and were making too many mistakes. In the second half CU scored touchdowns on a blocked punt and on an interception return to take a 17-6 lead, but the offense did little. A late CU field goal stretched the lead to 20-6, but Washington came back with a long touchdown and then threatened to tie the game in the last minute. With the Cougars on the CU 2-yard line, McChesney and Dizon combined to force a fumble. McChesney, whom the officials had admonished to "shut up" because of his trash talking early in the game, had spoken loudly without opening his mouth. He picked a perfect time to do it.

CU quarterback Joel Klatt then took a knee to kill the clock and the game was over. A little more sand was poured on the field. The Buffs now had a 2-0 record, but the press-box chatter again focused on their lack of offense. "They won't get away with this in the Big 12," one writer said.

He was right. They wouldn't get away with that in the Big 12. But, they had one more game to play before the Big 12 schedule. They had to fix what was wrong. And there were plenty of people willing to offer advice. They would need all the advice they could get before the conference schedule began.

In addition to a week-three game with undermanned North Texas before a bye week and a then trip to Missouri, the team would also have to continue dealing with the fallout from the 2001 party that started the scandal. In Boulder, the lingering heat of late-summer September would be nothing compared to the fires ignited by the party held on December 7, 2001.

Chapter Five
Day of Infamy

F all was officially a week away, but summer, like the allegations leveled at the CU football program, was still clinging to the foothills of Colorado like a wet football jersey.

Wet jerseys were easy to find when the University of Colorado football team broke practice on Sept. 16, two days before its third game of the season. The players practiced without full pads on Thursdays, but the heat and the surprising humidity took no break as the leaves began turning along Boulder Creek.

When practice finally ended, the CU players trudged up the steep path that crosses the creek and which separates the team's practice field from its stadium and locker room facility next to Folsom Field. The narrow path is closed to cars, but is heavily traveled by pedestrians and bicycle riders.

In spite of carrying nearly 300 pounds, Matt McChesney bounced up the hill. The heat, like almost everything else, didn't seem to bother him. During football season, it seemed, nothing could keep him from having a good time playing the game he loved. Later in the season he would fight off an ankle injury to practice in bitter cold on that same practice field.

"Can't beat this man," he would say of the lingering injury.

As he headed up the path in mid-September, he was reminded that not everyone shared his love of the game. A bicycle carrying a male student suddenly flew over the top of the hill, headed straight toward McChesney and several teammates. It was moving fast. The rider, with a defiant look on his face, didn't slow down and didn't turn. He was headed straight for the players. At the last second, McChesney and the others jumped out of the way. The bike rider flew by. There was no "excuse me." McChesney shook his head and resisted the temptation to yell something to the rider.

"Asshole," he grumbled to himself as he kept walking, ignoring the rider who seemed bent on starting an incident that would once again prove all those football players were really animals.

As a member of the CU football team, McChesney was no stranger to such abuse. In the past eight months his team had been referred to in the same sentence as the word "rape" more times than it could remember. Faculty members at CU had publicly claimed that too much importance was placed on football. Groups of female students had wandered the dormitory halls chanting anti-football slogans. The schism between CU's jocks and those who either didn't care about or just plain hated football had never been wider. In spite of two wins to start the season, the team had gotten very little respect from the sports media, either. An opportunistic defense, blocked kicks and a great place kicker—not an anemic offense—had carried the team, the newspapers said. The offense hadn't scored since the first quarter of the Colorado State game and didn't score at all in a win against Washington State. The CU offense was supposed to get healthy on Saturday when the University of North Texas came to Boulder. After all, UNT had been beaten 65-0 by Texas the week before. Its top two running backs were injured. And the school was making the move from Division Two football to Division One, a move that almost always results in a series of painful beatings. The UNT game would be a coming-out party for CU. Or so it seemed.

While CU looked to run its early-season record to 3-0, it was a party held nearly three years before that loomed over the team. Those around the team didn't talk about that party out loud, but a lawsuit stemming from it had nearly everyone else talking and was still threatening to bring down the football program. As the

Buffs got ready to party at the expense of North Texas, consensus opinion held that both the program and coach Gary Barnett were on their last legs and that CU would never again be able to recruit the caliber of athlete that had taken the team to within a hair's breadth of playing for the national championship just three seasons earlier

That ill-fated, so-called "recruiting party" had been held during the best of times for CU, just a week after the football team beat Texas in the Big 12 Championship Game. With recruiting visits sandwiched in between that game and the upcoming Fiesta Bowl game against Oregon, the coaches were busy. Basking in the glow of their conference championship, the players were giddy. In retrospect, some were a little too giddy. Their attendance and conduct at that party would cost them scholarships, reputations and, in some cases, their football careers. Although accounts vary, somewhere around a dozen CU players and recruits would visit the party that night. CU coach Gary Barnett allowed the older players to supervise the high-school recruits and he got burned. While most recruiting trips do not produce such incidents, that one has caused CU's to change its rules and it no longer allows players, who are barely older than the recruits, to supervise them. That party was nearly the undoing of the CU program and the players who attended.

Some of the players would just stop in at the party for a while.

Others would stay too long.

The players who brought the recruits to the party screwed up badly and were punished by the loss of their scholarships for a year. The ones who stayed too long would have their young lives altered in a way they would never forget.

Although most were not yet 21 years old, some of the players drank before and during the party.

Others smoked pot.

One of them brought an open bottle of whisky and another, a joint of marijuana. Those were acts that could get them in trouble with both the law and a head coach prudish enough to have once declined an invitation to a pre-season All-America banquet because it was sponsored by *Playboy* Magazine. They would indeed suffer the wrath of both the law and their coach, but a darker cloud loomed. The district attorney, the media, victim advocates and total strangers would soon accuse them of perhaps the most violent, despicable act this side of murder.

Rape.

Although never charged with rape—to this date, four years later—those players would go from being college kids who partied too much and had casual sex with strangers to rapists. There was little they could do to defend themselves.

And there was that other unspoken matter.

Their alleged victims were white.

Anne Gilmore and her friends were no strangers to the party scene at CU, which, to the chagrin of the administration, annually ranked the school among the top party schools in the country. Fraternity parties were legendary and, in the fall of 2004, 18-year-old Lynn Gordon "Gordie" Bailey died after reportedly drinking a lethal amount of alcohol during an initiation at CU's Chi Psi house. This was after the university had already cracked down on fraternity binge drinking by initiating a "two-strikes" rule that called for the suspension of either entire fraternities or individual students upon a second alcohol violation, including underage drinking. In the case of Gordie Bailey's fraternity, the university didn't have to act. The national Psi Chi executive council shut down its CU chapter and made it "dormant," citing both what it called the chapter's repeated violations of university policy and the "unhealthy" Greek atmosphere it perceived at CU.

At Gilmore's sorority, the drinking started early on Dec. 7, 2001. In statements to police, Gilmore and her friends said they got up around 3 p.m. on that December Saturday and starting drinking an hour later. According to their statements to police, several of them left for a party at Lisa Simpson's apartment around 8 p.m. Once at Simpson's, they played a drinking game called "Power Hour." The game involves drinking a shot of beer every minute for an hour and those who can do it for 10 minutes are considered members of the Power Hour Century Club. According to witness statements given in the investigation that would follow the party, one of the girls had also invited CU defensive back Corey Alexander and some friends. Alexander and friends would bring with them two recruits, high school players visiting the campus as part of the recruiting process.

Various accounts agree that as the evening progressed most of the people at that party were getting drunk, especially those who played Power Hour. Gilmore, in a deposition in her 2002 lawsuit, would say that on a scale of 1-10, with 1 being sober and 10 being passed out, her inebriation level was "between 9 and 10."

Lisa Simpson, who in later deposition said she thought only a handful of players would be at the party and that she was annoyed that "25 or 30 people" showed up,   would, in that same deposition, say she was passed out and too drunk to say "no" when allegedly sexually attacked by unknown football players and recruits she could not identify.

There is certainly no doubt the party got pretty wild. CU running back Chris Brown, who now plays for the Tennessee Titans, stopped by and didn't like what he saw. He left after someone threw up on his coat. "It wasn't for me," Brown would later tell investigators. Brown's decision to leave was a good one. Events that were about to take place in one of the bedrooms would change the course of the University of Colorado and its athletic program.

Everyone in attendance said there was sexual activity going on in one of the bedrooms at Simpson's apartment, but that's just about the only point upon which they agreed. Gilmore admitted to engaging in "heavy petting" with one player, but another female witness said the two were engaged in what appeared to be consensual oral sex. It was Gilmore, according to statements given by her friends, who earlier in the day said she "hadn't gotten any" in a while and hoped to "get some" that night. Those statements said she even told her friends she had her eye on defensive end Marques Harris. "Gilmore and Harris had been dating," said one athletic department employee. "I had seen them together." The line between consensual and non-consensual sex had been blurred by memories made hazy by intoxication and resulted in wildly-divergent witness accounts.

Simpson told both the police and her lawyers that she couldn't identify her alleged attackers. Her version of the story, already clouded by her admitted intoxication, says she got up and threw the players out of the party after the alleged assaults. Both she and her friends told police she got up and cleaned vomit from the bathroom and, 90 minutes after allegedly being raped while passed-out-drunk, drove some partygoers home. According to a timeline established by the depositions and witness statements, Simpson drove a car less than two hours after being, by her own admission, passed-out drunk. Witnesses, however, cast doubt on her claim to have been passed out. One of her friends told police Simpson giggled when the friend came into the bedroom to retrieve her sweater, which the friend said was pinned under Simpson on the bed while she was having sex. Several witnesses said she also passed out condoms just before the bedroom incident.

While Simpson could not identify her attackers, the players later said they saw her having what they believed to be consensual sex with two recruits, Anthony Wright and David

Gray. Tight end Jesse Wallace, according to the group, exposed himself to Gilmore in hopes of having oral sex. Barnett, in a deposition for Simpson's lawsuit, would later say he believed there was "consensual sex in one room between four of our current players and two recruits and two young ladies." CU players Allen Mackey, Corey Alexander and Harris were also in that room, according to the players. Defensive back Clyde Surrell would later be identified as the fifth player in the room.

Simpson, according to police reports, drove with and at the urging of a friend to Boulder Community Hospital about 3 a.m. following the party. In her deposition, Simpson said she went to the hospital after arriving back at her apartment when "the events of that night began to sink in." She said she told a female friend, "These people had sex with me, and I didn't know they were having sex with me," adding, "They had sex without my consent, and I didn't know who had done it, and I didn't know how many people had sex with me, and I was very upset, and I was crying, and I was very traumatized."

According to notes taken by the duty nurse and introduced in Simpson's deposition, she reported remembering "having sexual vaginal intercourse with one person and oral intercourse with one or two other people." In her deposition, Simpson said she was "positive" she never told the nurse she had intercourse with one person. Simpson, who stated she initially went to the hospital because she feared sexually-transmitted diseases and possibly pregnancy, was given a standard rape examination and was tested for sexually-transmitted diseases after telling the nurse she believed she was the victim of non-consensual sex.

Police reports said that, prior to the party, several recruits and players smoked pot and drank Seagram's 7 and Bacardi rum in a dorm room shared by Harris and Alexander in the Stearns East complex. Those reports said Gray and Alexander had a drinking contest that resulted in Gray throwing up. Gray, when interviewed by police at his Texas home, would say the players bragged to him that alcohol and sex were available "every weekend" to Big 12 champion CU players.

Gray, during a police interview in which he admitted having consensual sex with Simpson, also said Mackey and Alexander were running around naked at the party. When given a CU media guide with pictures of all the players, he identified wide receiver Ron Monteilh as the one who brought a marijuana joint to the party. That identification would later be proved false, but it didn't help Monteilh. Four months after the party, Monteilh, Mackey, Harris and Alexander would be charged with felony contribution to the delinquency of a minor. Three years later District Attorney Mary Keenan's office would file only misdemeanor charges against those believed to have supplied the alcohol consumed by fraternity pledge Gordie Bailey before he died.

But the black players who attended the Simpson party were in big trouble long before charges were filed at the end of April 2002. Barnett, who heard of the incident when someone gave him a copy of a *Boulder Daily Camera* story five days after the party, went ballistic almost immediately. He called a meeting of the 10-12 players who attended the party, but by all accounts he was the only one doing the talking as the meeting infolded. "Initially that meeting was a one-way conversation, and with me doing most of the talking and yelling," he said in his deposition. "It was not a quiet meeting. I was really angry. And I told them, informed them, that they were going to tell me everything that happened and they were going to tell me the truth; and if they didn't tell me the truth there would be hell to pay. And most of my players know that if they'll tell me the truth, you know, they'll get a fair shake, but if they don't, then I won't have anything to do with them. And so I was pretty sure that I got the truth."

After that two-hour tongue-lashing, which players later also described as largely a one-sided conversation, their coach called the players' parents.

"I made a point to tell each of them that they were minimally going to lose their scholarship, and that they needed an attorney for their son, and then made sure they knew what was going on, or what happened at the party, what their son's role was, and that I was disgusted," Barnett said in his deposition in the Simpson case.

Convinced that the players had not committed rape, but livid that their stupidity had violated team rules and brought shame to the program, Barnett was true to his vow to revoke scholarships. He pulled the scholarships of Wallace, Harris, Mackey and Alexander for the spring semester. Wallace and Harris stayed in school, while Mackey transferred to Sacramento State and Alexander transferred to South Texas.

Those four would eventually plead guilty to misdemeanor charges of contributing to the delinquency of a minor. Clyde Surrell would later clear Monteilh's name by going to campus police and identifying himself as the one who brought the joint to the party. Surrell was issued a citation for possession of marijuana, a petty offense carrying a maximum $100 fine, but prosecutors in District Attorney Mary Keenan's office balked at the deal. Unless Surrell pleaded guilty to the same charge as the other four, they said, he would be charged with other crimes. Already facing expulsion from school for undisclosed disciplinary problems not associated with the party, Surrell took the deal. There was no need for Barnett to take away his scholarship. Surrell had exhausted his eligibility and was already gone.

While he was angry about his players' conduct on the night of the party, Barnett also had reason to believe that none of his players raped Simpson. None of the four were connected to the incident by DNA tests—a fact that, in spite of its importance to the story, has never been reported in the media.

Keenan, in announcing there would be no rape charges, said she believed Simpson was raped, but cited "identity problems" that precluded the filing of charges. Identity problems, however, didn't stop her from charging Monteilh with contributing to the delinquency of a minor on a single shred of evidence, Gray's erroneous identification of him from pictures in the team media guide.

Gray eventually chose to attend the University of California at Berkley and CU eventually dropped its pursuit of Anthony Wright. But Boulder authorities didn't drop their pursuit of the CU football program. Boulder Police Chief Mark Beckner, in a May interview with the *Boulder Daily Camera*, defended the decision to not file charges against the women who provided alcohol at the party. Beckner told the paper that if police had charged everyone they wouldn't have had any witnesses and that authorities chose to charge only the most serious offenses. Beckner said the players were targeted not because of their race, but because they were in charge of the recruits. Two years later Beckner, who had publicly cleared "suspects" in the infamous JonBenet Ramsey murder case, refused to clear any players, saying that while it is not uncommon to clear rape suspects who have been exonerated, "I don't think that is the case here."

Keenan didn't give up on the case with the no-file decision of early 2002. In February of 2004 she told the *Daily Camera* she had enlisted the aid of three Boulder-area investigators to pore over the dozens of depositions given in Simpson's civil case in hopes of finding additional evidence, since under Colorado law rape charges could be filed up to 10 years after the fact. Apparently no such evidence has been found. Months after the filing of charges against the players and after being criticized for her apparently-dual roles in the criminal and civil cases, she surrendered the criminal investigation to Colorado Attorney General Ken Salazar's office following several days of rumor that governor Bill Owens was going to ask Salazar to take over the ongoing criminal investigation. Keenan made an announcement that she had decided to turn over the criminal side of the probe voluntarily.

Although Simpson's admittedly alcohol-fogged memory precluded her from identifying her alleged assailants, entries in her personal diary indicated she was happy about the punishment of the players. When she gave her deposition in December of 2003, almost exactly a year after filing her suit, she seemed ready to blame the CU players who had been charged with contributing to the delinquency of minors. Lawyers for CU confronted her with passages from that diary in which she said, "God help me, I will ruin the lives of Joseph Allen Mackey, Marques Harris, Corey Alexander, Ron Monteilh, Jesse Wallace and whoever the recruits are." Simpson had earlier and repeatedly said she could not identify her alleged attackers. When reminded of that fact during the deposition, she said she was glad that players she could not identify were being punished.

"I was happy that someone who was in that room who either raped me or allowed me to be raped was getting punished for their actions, and they should have been punished because they were contributing to minors anyway." When reminded that she, too, contributed to the delinquency of minors, her reply was short.

"That's true,' she said.

It was also true that a white male friend of Simpson had purchased for her a case of Keystone beer for the party. While unable to remember in the deposition if she ever discussed the alcohol purchase with that man, he, in another deposition, admitted buying her the beer and said he and Simpson discussed leaving his name out of the case so that he wouldn't get in trouble. Some might see that as some sort of obstruction of justice, but it turns out he had nothing to worry about. Authorities knew his name but never charged him.

Simpson's deposition also revealed another part of her diary that made it understandable why her attorney called me in a rage when I obtained portions quoted in her deposition. "It gave me so much pleasure to know that these assholes were going to be arrested and to know that this is something that would follow them forever," she wrote. "Even though they are not arrested for sexual assault, they are arrested."

Karen Burd, Simpson's mother, said in a deposition that her daughter hadn't thought of filing a civil suit until Keenan advised her of her right to do so. Burd said Keenan's advice didn't cause her daughter to file the suit, but that it began the thought process that led to that decision. In her own deposition, Simpson said she didn't think of suing the university until Keenan brought it up in a February 2002 meeting requested by Keenan.

Gilmore's path to federal court was longer than Simpson's, but her suit, filed almost exactly a year later in December of 2003, was nearly identical. Her story, however, had taken on a different form by the time the suit was filed. Gilmore, who earlier told police she had consensual sexual contact with a player at the party and didn't claim to have been raped, now claimed she was raped "by a football player" after she got drunk and passed out at the party after dancing with two players in a bedroom. But her actions prior to the filing of the suit raise questions.

According to police report written by Boulder detective Melissa Kampf, Gilmore told her she approached *Daily Camera* columnist Neil Woelk two days after the party in order to expose CU's alleged recruiting practices and the resultant "gang rape" at the December 7 party. Kampf's report, however, goes on to say that Gilmore, "later told me she embellished what she had seen because she wanted the reporter to take her seriously and write an article about the CU recruiting program." In March of 2005 Woelk said that when Gilmore approached him days after the party, she denied being raped.

The timing of Gilmore's suit was also interesting. It was filed a week after she gave a deposition in Simpson's suit. Her attorney, Peggy Jessel, told the *Daily Camera* the deposition convinced her to file the suit. The *Camera* story quoted Jessel as saying the intensity of questioning, which lasted seven hours, was overwhelming for Gilmore. The suit was also the first time Gilmore mentioned being raped. When interviewed by police in April 2002 she didn't mention it. She didn't make the allegations in her deposition, either. It was not until she filed her suit that she claimed to have had forced sexual contact with at least two men. The suit doesn't mention her earlier admission to having consensual sex with a player. There were certainly different versions of her story, but fear of insensitivity apparently kept the media from reporting the discrepancies. But, just as it is wrong to reject all rape claims out of hand, it must surely be just as wrong to assume all rape claims are valid. The media never sought to find that balance, instead choosing to inflame public opinion based on a lawsuit that would eventually be thrown out of court.

A third woman, former CU soccer player Monique Gillaspie, also filed a suit claiming she was raped by a football player she picked up at a Boulder bar after the party. Her suit claimed she had some consensual contact with the player, but that he forced himself on her when she decided to stop the sexual encounter. Gillaspie abruptly dropped her suit in late 2004, but by then it didn't seem to matter to the media or the public it pretends to serve. The damage had long ago been done. The reputation of the CU football team was in tatters. The CU administration, in spite of having reinstated Barnett after a four-month suspension and in spite of having in hand an investigative report saying the football program had not condoned the use of sex and alcohol, had done nearly nothing to defend its football program.

"It's because of political correctness," one longtime CU employee said. "It's politically incorrect to question any accusation involving sexual assault. They were afraid of being called insensitive."

It was a little late for that.

Within minutes of the May 2004 press conference at which CU president Elizabeth Hoffman reinstated Barnett with a less-than ringing endorsement of his character, Regina Cowles, the director of the Boulder chapter of the National Organization of Women, blasted Hoffman in front of reporters. It was clear she wanted Barnett fired. "These actions on the part of CU President Elizabeth Hoffman make her a full-fledged member of the good ol' boys club," an angry Cowles said. "Her loyalty to the coach and athletic director is not in the best interest of the university." Cowles couldn't have mischaracterized Hoffman's relationship with Barnett and athletic director Dick Tharp any more had she tried. Tharp would be forced out of his job before another football season ended. Some athletic department employees privately claimed Hoffman, lacking the funds to pay off the nearly $6 million left on Barnett's contract if he were fired, instituted severe academic and recruiting restrictions on the program in order to force him to throw up his hands and quit. It became clear that if Hoffman was a member of the good ol' boys club, her membership was forced. Tharp and Barnett were definitely not her boys.

By mid-2002 no one could argue that players who attended the December 7 party had not been punished. They had been punished by the law—some say singled out—by a district attorney they claimed had it in for the program.

"There is very little that would make you believe these four young men (Monteilh, Mackey, Alexander and Wallace) had any sexual contact, consensual or otherwise, with the alleged victim," said Boulder attorney Sonny Flowers, who represented Mackey.

Flowers said the evidence points to contact only by two recruits who never enrolled at CU and fails to show that it was non-consensual. He also blasted authorities for failing to clear the four after DNA tests failed to produce evidence connecting them to the incident.

The players were also punished by their coach with loss of their scholarships. While Mackey and Alexander transferred almost immediately, Wallace had to pay his own tuition to stay in school the rest of that year. So did Harris, who, when the case was suddenly rekindled two years later, transferred to Southern Utah after a second suspension. The transfer of Harris left Wallace as the only charged player on the roster. Wallace was never accused of rape, bringing the total number of current CU players suspected of sex assault to zero. That fact meant little to the opposing fans who would chant "rapists" at the CU bench during games. It was the release of Keenan's deposition, coupled with what I believe was the media's blind allegiance to Simpson's press agent, that would re-light that fire in early 2004.

Wallace and his teammates were trying to light a fire of a different sort as they prepared for their third game of the 2004 season. Aside from Bobby Purify's running, the Buffs' offense had been nearly non-existent in wins over Colorado State and Washington State. Barnett, in an attempt to stoke that fire, placed the words "Shovel the Coal" on the front of the weekly itinerary handout. Keep shoveling the coal, he told his players, and the fire would blaze. When Washington State held Purify to only 53 net yards, that fire nearly went out. The players, however, didn't need any more heat as they prepared to take the field against North Texas. Although the game was played at 5 p.m., the temperature was still a muggy 87 degrees. Early in the game it looked as though the only fire was going to be supplied by the Mean Green of North Texas.

Using a 57-yard run by third-string tailback Jamario Thomas, who was placed in the starting lineup only when two other players sustained injuries, North Texas jumped in to the lead before Bobby Purify's 11-yard run tied the game. The unknown running back, however, would score again on a day during which he would finish with 247 yards and gave UNT the lead again. Purify scored the second of his three touchdowns to tie the game in the second quarter and CU wouldn't look back en route to a 52-21 victory. Supposedly-undermanned North Texas had torched CU for over 500 yards. It wasn't exactly a great tune up for the upcoming Big 12 season.

Despite the fact that CU's offense had lit up North Texas as it was supposed to, there was no party atmosphere in the locker room after the win. While the offense had shown its first real life of the season, the defense had given up a whopping 507 yards. Thomas, who was not even expected to play in the game, had recorded the second most rushing yards ever given up by CU in one game, second only to the 268 yards gained by Kansas tailback David Winbush in 1998.

Linebacker Akarika Dawn spoke for the entire defense after the game.

"We were bad," he said. "We messed up a lot. As you saw, they broke a couple of long ones on us. It wasn't what they did, it was what we did."

Barnett, in spite of being 3-0, wasn't happy either.

"We weren't as sharp as we should have been, or as sharp as we need to be and that's all I'm going to say about it," he said.

The coaches seemed happy just to have a bye week coming up. They would now have two weeks to prepare their players for their first Big 12 game, a road game at Missouri. CU's 3-0 record would be tested mightily in Columbia, the home of the team most analysts had picked to win the Big 12 North.

CU had completed one fourth of the season that followed what Barnett had once called a "Pearl Harbor" attack on his program. The fans in Missouri were not about to let CU forget about December 7, 2001.

Chapter Six
"She Was a Girl"

ollege football stadiums, perhaps more than most large
structures, take on a different air when empty. A single
human voice echoes in the emptiness that only hours
before reverberated the voices of thousands.

On game day full parking lots and large crowds turn stadiums
into compacted cities often larger than those in which they are
located.

During halftime, crowds line the hallways leading to over-
crowded restrooms.

Over-priced, mostly bad, food is available everywhere, along
with some form of local cuisine dictated by regional culture:

Burritos at the University of New Mexico.

Bratwursts at Wisconsin.

Buffalo burgers at the University of Colorado.

A full stadium is a concessionaire's dream. Where else can
they get people to shell out for over-priced soft drinks and beer to
wash down nachos made of that fake cheese?

An empty stadium is another story. Especially in the early
morning.

I had been an embedded journalist with the CU football team
for three weeks when I drove into Boulder just before dawn three
days after the University of Colorado's 52-21 win over North
Texas. Only a few coaches' cars dotted the parking lot next to the
Dal Ward Center attached to the south end of the stadium. The
Dal Ward Center was almost as empty as the stadium.

Dal Ward, named after a former CU football coach, is usually
not an exciting place. Athletic department employees go about
their business in the building that houses all the sports programs
upstairs and the locker rooms downstairs. Trophies earned in

various sports are dotted throughout the building and a massive trophy case forms the front of the second-floor weight room. Motivational slogans share wall space with plaques identifying donors who paid for a particular room or bench or trophy case. Student-athletes come and go throughout the day. Occasionally the steps leading to the main entrance serve as the location for impromptu press conferences.

As I drove up the steep, narrow driveway on that late-September morning, the Dal Ward Center seemed deathly quiet. Looking up at the empty steps at the main entrance, I remembered a day seven months ago when those steps were neither empty nor quiet.

Like September 21, February 17, 2004 was a Tuesday. For CU coach Gary Barnett, it would turn into Black Tuesday. It was the day *Sports Illustrated* rocked the sports world with a column by Rick Reilly, a CU graduate who had nine times been named the national sportswriter of the year and who wrote a weekly humor column at the back of the magazine.

This particular column, however, was anything but funny. Neither was the impromptu afternoon press conference Barnett held on those Dal Ward Center steps just after the issue hit the stands. His words at that conference would be the last he uttered as CU's football coach for three months. Barnett would be suspended the next day for the sin of political incorrectness, placing his professional future in doubt.

Reilly's article would hurdle Colorado's biggest story into the national spotlight.

The headline on Reilly's column referenced another victim at CU, using the word "another" to imply that there had been others. The column, however, never specifically mentioned any others.

Calling CU's recruiting parties "jailbreaks", Reilly's column dropped another bombshell on the beleaguered program. Kicker Katie Hnida, a former homecoming queen and place kicker at

suburban Chatfield High School near Denver, claimed she had
been raped by a CU teammate in the summer of 2000. Hnida
made news in 1999 when former coach Rick Neuheisel invited
her to join the team as a non-scholarship walk-on. Neuheisel,
however, left in January 1999 and was replaced by Barnett.

According to Reilly's column, Hnida was at the home of a
teammate in August 2000 when the teammate, against her
wishes, started kissing her and making other advances. The
player, according to Hnida, forced himself on her, later stopping
his assault to get up and pick up a ringing telephone. She didn't
report the incident to police, she told Reilly, because she was
afraid of what her attacker, a man who outweighed her by 100
pounds, might do to her and because she wanted to avoid what
she called a giant media mess. Hnida, in the column, went on to
accuse her former teammates of a litany of crude behavior that
included verbal harassment, lewd propositions, indecent
exposure and groping. Reilly quoted former teammate Justin
Bates as saying Hnida endured more abuse than any person
should endure. Bates later said his comments were taken out of
context and that he meant that Hnida wasn't respected by the
other players. He also said he knew nothing of a sexual assault.

Reilly also interviewed another player, but inexplicably
didn't quote him in the article. That player, former lineman
Anwaan Jones, had played for Barnett both at Northwestern and
Colorado and has been employed as a police officer in Oakland,
California, since graduating. He described himself as one of
Hnida's best friends on the team and said the two spent time
together off the field. "We used to visit when we were standing
on the sideline at practice, too," he said shortly after the *Sports
Illustrated* story came out. Jones' side of the story, however,
didn't make it into Reilly's blockbuster. "I think (Reilly) played
me," Jones said. "I told him that I never saw anything that was
alleged, but he didn't use my quotes." A story carrying

allegations of that magnitude had left out the eyewitness account of a player who was close to Hnida, but whose story didn't match Reilly's.

And *Sports Illustrated* printed it.

Reilly stretched the truth in his column when he said the CU situation made him, as an alumnus of the school, want to hide his class ring. He later admitted to a member of the CU staff that he had never purchased a class ring.

When I interviewed Jones by phone days later, he admitted that most of his teammates did, indeed, disrespect Hnida. "Katie was a good person and I would never demean her character," he said, "but guys disrespected her because she wasn't good enough to kick at a Division One school. The same goes for male players. Guys ridicule them if they are not good enough to be in this program. Is that right? Probably not. But that's the way it is. That's just football."

The Hnida situation was further clouded by her own alleged conduct during the year she played for CU. When the *Sports Illustrated* article hit the stands, several current and former players came forth and offered to tell what they knew of Hnida. They said she had dated several players. They claimed she was a willing participant in the vulgar, sophomoric humor that is evident inside most locker rooms. They even said Hnida exposed her breasts at a post-game party in a hot tub following the Insight.com Bowl played in Tucson at the end of the 2000 season. Hnida brushed aside a question about that incident during a 2005 interview on the *Today Show* and the truth about her stay at CU will probably never be known. Her conduct, in my mind was not even relevant. Most college students do things they are later not proud of and it doesn't matter if it happened or not. While the personal life of Hnida or anyone else would normally be no one's business, in this case it seemed to be relevant to her accusations of unilateral vulgar, unwanted harassment by teammates. It didn't seem relevant, however, to the reporters who only reported one side of the story. It was politically incorrect to question Hnida's allegations.

CU considered revealing what players had said about Hnida's past. Barnett, in fact, e-mailed athletic director Dick Tharp on the day the article came out, asking "how aggressive should I be re: Katie" in reference to "sexual conquests by her, etc." CU officials briefly flirted with the idea of defending themselves, but ultimately decided the school's staggering image problems would only get worse if it took the politically-incorrect step of countering Hnida's allegations. They were right. They would perhaps be more damned if they spoke about Hnida than if they said nothing. It was a no-win situation.

Barnett never got a written answer from Tharp, according to e-mails later released by the university. He never got the chance. Barnett's comments on the steps of the Dal Ward Center later that Tuesday would undermine that opportunity. While addressing the Hnida situation in a hastily-called news conference, he was repeatedly asked if his players disrespected Hnida because of her gender or because of her kicking abilities. Barnett at first seemed to avoid addressing her kicking abilities, but finally answered the question.

It was a bad decision, given the circumstances.

"Katie was a girl," he said. "Not only was she a girl, she was terrible. There's no other way to say it. She couldn't kick the ball through the uprights."

Television news reports endlessly re-played that portion of the interview without re-playing the questions leading up to it. They made it appear as though Barnett was saying it was okay to sexually abuse the young woman because she was a bad kicker. He didn't say that, but it didn't matter. He was in big trouble. Hours later he would be in bigger trouble when the university and the media were given copies of a 2001 police report in which a part-time athletic department employee claimed to have been raped by a player. The woman did not file charges against the player, but her police report claimed Barnett swore to back the player "100 percent" if she pressed charges. The report didn't mention that Barnett met with both the woman and the player and made the player apologize for what he considered to be crude conduct.

It was all too much for CU president Elizabeth Hoffman, whose school was being leveled daily by new reports of sexual misconduct. The next day, Wednesday, she called a 10 p.m. press conference that was to be held at CU's offices in downtown Denver. Speculation in the media ran wild. Why would the university call a 10 p.m. news conference? Was it to announce Barnett's firing on the 10 o'clock news? Reporters scrambling to the press conference were certain that Hoffman was going to announce his termination. Outside the building, *Boulder Daily Camera* columnist Neil Woelk said his sources told him Barnett was going to be suspended. Woelk was right.

Hoffman announced that Barnett had been placed on paid suspension and that his fate would be decided after the completion of both an internal investigation and an investigative committee's final report. "We will make some kind of determination at that time," she said of the dual investigations that were supposed to be completed by April but which would stretch into May. Hoffman also assailed Barnett's comment about Hnida.

"Those comments were inappropriate in the context of a sexual assault," she said. Just over a year later, her stance on free speech would change radically. On February 22, 2005, she warned the Colorado Legislature that attempts to fire CU ethnic studies professor Ward Churchill, the author of an essay in which he likened the World Trade Center terror-attack victims to Nazis, would backfire and result in lawsuits that would make Churchill a wealthy man. An Associated Press story quoted Hoffman as saying the law protects public employees' right to free speech, regardless of how odious that speech might be. Apparently Churchill's reference to the "technocrats" in the World Trade Center as "little Eichmanns" was not as bad as Barnett's insensitivity to a place kicker. While Hoffman publicly intimated the university couldn't afford to fire Churchill, she had never mentioned the multi-million dollar price tag that would have come with Barnett's firing. In fact, during the press conference to announce Barnett's reinstatement, she talked tough and said that if any allegations were proven, she "wouldn't be afraid to fire people." She would be a little more afraid to fire Churchill.

The late-night February press conference to announce Barnett's suspension also put a stake in the hearts of die-hard CU football fans. Chancellor Richard Byyny, who has since retired, told reporters that "winning and losing is not an issue" anymore at CU. University officials seemed ready to put the football program and its coach to rest for good. In that same press conference, Hoffman said the university was also "utterly distressed by the information contained in the (2001 police) report." She added, "We have not acted in haste" in suspending Barnett. Hoffman would later say she erred in thinking Barnett's comments were made regarding the possible sexual assault, not in the context of his being asked repeatedly about Hnida's ability.

CU officials would quickly move to install longtime assistant coach Brian Cabral as the team's "interim coach," a title he would hold through spring football and into mid-May.

Barnett spent most of that night at his Boulder office in the Dal Ward Center, where athletic director Dick Tharp had earlier delivered the news of his suspension. As he walked to his car after the press conference, Barnett read a statement to reporters in which he said his comments the day before "were either misinterpreted or taken clearly taken out of context." An examination of the entire interview shows his argument to be true. While he disparaged Hnida's kicking abilities, he did not do so within the context of a sexual assault. He said it in response to a specific, repeated question about her abilities. It was clearly the media that connected the two subjects.

"What I wanted to communicate is that, regardless of Katie's kicking abilities, I wanted Katie on our football team," he said. "I wanted to give her a chance to be part of this program." Barnett went on to say he was "very sensitive" to Hnida's allegations and added, "I want to do whatever I can to help Katie." Barnett said Hnida's presence gave his team "diversity." It also allowed the team to carry one more male player under the complicated federal Title IX regulations dictating parity between men's and women's sports.

While Hnida claimed sexual harassment was part of her daily experience on the CU football team, Barnett—in his deposition on the Simpson case—said he knew of only one such incident. That 1999 incident, brought to his attention by Hnida's father, David, involved then-backup quarterback Zac Colvin. Colvin had reportedly called Hnida a "cunt." Barnett said he immediately sought out Colvin and gave him what he described as a "tongue-lashing." According to that deposition, David Hnida, who is also known as "Dr. Dave" on a local television station where he gives health advice, contacted Barnett again the following summer to tell him the verbal abuse by Colvin had not stopped.

"(David Hnida) told me that whatever I used to discipline (Colvin) didn't work because he had continued to name-call his daughter," Barnett said in the deposition, adding that he had a second conversation with Colvin, who denied continuing the verbal abuse. David Hnida, who by the spring of 2004 was serving as an army doctor in Iraq, would on March 30 send the investigative committee an e-mail saying he was "distressed" by statements Barnett and the university had made, statements that displayed "quite a bit of lying and deception."

Neither David Hnida nor his daughter testified before the commission, which on May 18 issued a report that had been leaked to the *Rocky Mountain News* a day earlier. The report, while saying there was no evidence CU coaches sanctioned or had any role in the infamous "recruiting party," blasted CU administrators for what it called lax oversight of the athletic department. It blamed Chancellor Richard Byyny and Athletic Director Dick Tharp for not instituting recruiting changes called for in 1998.

With the exception of her cooperation with Reilly for his column, Hnida has since given only one media interview, a taped conversation with Katie Couric that was broadcast on NBC's *Today Show* on January 10 and 11 of 2005. While introducing Hnida, Couric made reference to allegations of 10 rapes involving the CU football team. I had been covering the story for over two years and couldn't up come with that many accusations, let alone credible allegations. Innuendo had by now combined with speculation to inflate the number of un-named, un-charged rapists on the CU football team to 10.

During the interview Couric, like the Denver TV stations before her, played only the last part of Barnett's now-infamous statement before asking Hnida to comment. Hnida seized on the comments, saying they reflected the way Barnett treated her while she was at CU. In the second part of the interview, Couric briefly and almost apologetically mentioned the allegations that Hnida had exposed herself in that hot tub at the Insight.com Bowl. Calling those allegations unbelievable, Hnida said that while she didn't mind being criticized as a kicker, such allegations were despicable to her.

Hnida's allegations of intolerable conditions for women, however, came as news to a woman who shared a locker room with her in the CU athletic department and who also served as a rape counselor and victim advocate. Megan Rogers, who now works as an administrative assistant for CU defensive coordinator Mike Hankwitz and offensive coordinator Shawn Watson, got perhaps the closest look at Hnida's experience at CU. Rogers, an undergraduate assistant equipment manager who later became a rape-crisis hotline volunteer, shared a locker room with the school's first and only female football player. She remembers things differently.

"We conversed every day," Rogers said, "getting ready for practice, seeing her after practice." Hnida, according to Rogers, never mentioned being harassed.

"I know people can keep things inside them." Rogers said. "Maybe she was just a good actress and kept it all in, but I was a psychology major and I never saw anything that made me believe something was bothering her. The only time I remember her being down was when she was getting mono(nucleosis) and complained of being tired." Rogers said she never saw or experienced the harassment Hnida would later allege.

"The accusation about (Katie) being cornered by players outside her locker room is strange," she said. "I used that locker room and didn't see anything. If that stuff was happening to her, why wasn't it happening to me?" Rogers said she "never once" experienced verbal or physical harassment from a player. She said Hnida seemed to be friends with and "talked about hanging out" with male players. Although she had no idea at the time, Rogers' relationship to Hnida would later place her under a brief-but intense media spotlight and would cost her volunteer job at a rape-crisis center.

While applying to graduate school at CU, Rogers decided to volunteer as a counselor for Moving to End Sexual Assault, or MESA, a Boulder organization that ran a rape-crisis hotline. After undergoing what she called a "pretty intense" 40-hour training session, she began volunteering three 12-hour shifts per month as an on-call counselor. When reporters learned of her relationship to Hnida, they started asking her questions. MESA didn't like her answers—one that included, "Katie never discussed any of these issues with me," and "Nothing remotely like that happened to me."

Rogers said her supervisors at MESA asked her how she would have handled a call from Hnida alleging rape by a teammate. "I told them I would have handled it like any other call," she said. That wasn't good enough for those who ran MESA. "After a series of phone calls, they told me they thought I was too close to the situation; I couldn't be objective. They said my comments were victim-blaming." Finally, Rogers said, "They told me I should take a break for a while. They never called me back."

Rogers testified before the investigative committee, but her testimony got little media play. The testimony of MESA director Janine D'Anniballe, however, got plenty. Headlines blared her allegation that MESA had in the past three months gotten two more calls from women accusing CU players of rape. D'Anniballe refused to provide more details, citing the organization's policy of confidentiality. That policy didn't, however, keep her from publicly accusing un-named players of rape while offering nothing to substantiate the allegations. The media had no problem broadcasting those new allegations based solely on D'Anniballe's nebulous statement.

"I was a little bit frustrated by her testifying that MESA had gotten two recent calls accusing CU players of rape," Rogers said of D'Anniballe's testimony. "MESA has a policy of confidentiality and she breached it. They breached their own policy of not confiding information about either end of a call."

The Hnida allegations are unlikely to go away. According to the *Today Show*, Hnida, who graduated from the University of New Mexico after becoming the first female to kick an extra point in a Division One football game, is pursuing possible book and movie deals. The rift between David Hnida and CU also remains curious. Sources confirmed that after his daughter left CU, Doctor Dave contacted athletic officials outside the football department to suggest that CU take a look at his son, a linebacker at Chatfield High School in suburban Denver.

The extent of Katie Hnida's harassment at CU will likely never be known. We will probably never find all the answers to the questions the media has failed to ask. One fact, however, is indisputable.

The media hasn't even started looking.

During my three months with the football team, I never saw or heard of behavior resembling that described by Hnida. Female assistant trainers and staff members were treated with respect and the players seemed interested in little else but football. The players were business-like and were, for the most part, quiet. Even the handful of profanely-vocal players, such as Matt McChesney and Lawrence Vickers, never swore in the presence of women. Not a week went by in which Barnett didn't remind his players that he expected them to be gentlemen—a practice that, according to the players, began before the scandal broke and long before I started sitting in on the team meetings. If the attitudes in the football program described by Hnida existed when she was at CU, there is absolutely no evidence they exist now. Could Barnett have reeled in an out-of-control program that quickly in the face of the allegations? Could a bunch of thugs start acting like gentlemen overnight because the world was watching them?

The fact that neither investigators nor reporters had substantiated the allegations against CU, the media's thirst for scandal—real or imagined—didn't stop.

By the time I had been with the team for a few weeks, I was starting to receive a great lesson in how the media craves dirty laundry, just like in that classic Don Henley song, *Dirty Laundry*. A fellow reporter had already called me telling me that one of my editors was disappointed in the series I was writing. "I wish he would write stuff that would piss those fuckers off," the editor had said within earshot of the reporter. Those "fuckers' meant CU. I naively thought my editors wanted me to write what I saw. What they really wanted, I came to realize, was more scandal. Even if it wasn't there. I thought about that as I pulled into the parking lot on the cold, rainy morning of September 21. Compared to that Tuesday in February this morning was a ray of sunshine, I thought.

It was quiet.

There were lots of parking spaces at 6:30 a.m.

There were no microphones and cameras on the front steps. CU was enjoying a respite from the recurrent storms of what was by now commonly called The CU Recruiting Scandal.

It seemed almost everyone in Boulder was still sleeping as the sky began to lighten. Only the Denver-Boulder Turnpike, lined with the ribbon of southbound headlights formed by commuters heading into Denver, displayed any signs of life. At Folsom Field the only sound came from a noisy pair of raccoons foraging under the stands in the south end of the stadium as if hoping the cleaning crew had missed a morsel of fake cheese or a chunk of buffalo-burger bun.

The raccoons were facing slim pickings in a stadium scheduled to be empty for the next three weeks. CU was on a bye week before traveling to Missouri to open the Big 12 season and wouldn't return to Folsom Field until the Oklahoma State game on Oct. 9. But there was no mistaking a bye week for an off week. School and football would still dictate nearly every move the players made.

"They won't get any time off," Barnett said after the North Texas game. "Well, I guess they'll get Saturday off, since we don't have a game. Otherwise, the week will be just like every other week."

The freshmen probably didn't want to hear that. Their chance of sleeping in that week went down the tubes when Barnett told them they would still have to report to "Breakfast Club," a euphemism for a mandatory breakfast at 7 a.m. on Monday through Thursday. Since coming to CU five seasons before, Barnett had required freshman attendance at Breakfast Club. Intern coaches or graduate assistants also attended, marking off names on a clipboard as the players dragged themselves in. On a cold morning in later September, Breakfast Club looked much like the morning detention sessions in the John Hughes movie from which the phrase was taken.

Sewell Hall, the home of the Breakfast Club, was only a couple hundred yards west of Folsom Field. But it seemed a million miles from the noisy, crowded campus of three days ago. The only cheery presence in Sewell Hall was the loud voice of A.J., a middle-aged black woman who worked in the dining hall and on early mornings doubled as sort of a maitre d'. I grabbed a cup of coffee and waited for the players.

"Hey, baby. How you doin'?'" she said as the first players came in around 6:45 a.m..

"Morning, baby. Let me get a towel to dry you off."

A.J. had already gotten to know the freshmen and seemed to take delight in making them her own kids four mornings a week

Linebacker Jordan Dizon came in wearing clothes that would have been more appropriate in his home state of Hawaii. Sandals didn't quite make it on the first days of fall, but Dizon's appetite seemed unaffected. He made a giant McMuffin-looking sandwich from a split bagel, a pile of scrambled eggs, cheese and two sausage links. Dizon, who had surprisingly earned a starting linebacker spot and had become the team's leading tackler as a true freshman, wasn't done yet. He took a second plate and piled it with ham, hash browns and more sausage. After washing it all down with two glasses of apple juice, he quickly took his tray back to the kitchen and grabbed a donut on his way out the door. Defensive back Corey Reid, who looked skinny at 185 pounds, downed a breakfast larger than the one Dizon had just inhaled. "I'm going to need this food for all day," he told his teasing larger teammates.

Linebacker Drew Ford didn't even notice the cold as he came in. He had grown up in the small town of Alamosa, which is generally regarded as one of the coldest towns in Colorado, or the nation for that matter. "I wish it got this warm in Alamosa," he laughed. Ford, who brought his books to Breakfast Club, said he thought the mandatory breakfast was a good idea. "Especially for freshmen," he said. "A lot of times you want to go back to bed. If I do, I'm going to miss class. I know it helps me."

It apparently didn't help everyone. Intern coach Darian Hagan, who had been the quarterback during CU's national championship run in 1989, was babysitting Breakfast Club that morning and scowled as he looked down at his clipboard. There were a couple guys missing. Hagan reached for his cell phone.

"Get your ass over here," he half whispered into the phone. After a pause, he spoke into the phone again.

"I don't care if you don't have your shoes with you. Walk fast –it's wet out there."

Hagan didn't want to put any names on the list. He would rather call his sleeping freshmen than put their names on a list that would earn them a spot in a place much worse than Breakfast Club.

A place called Commitment Time.

Commitment Time was new that year, although punishment by Barnett for missing meals or classes was not. Prisoners of Commitment Time had to report to the Dal Ward Center on Saturday night at 10 and had to stay until 2 a.m. If they had missed class the presiding graduate assistant would likely make them hit the books during four of the few free hours they had each week. Strength coach Greg Finnegan, who among the CU coaches is the equivalent of Strother Martin's character in "Cool Hand Luke," had recently made the Commitment Time players push a blocking sled up and down Folsom Field in the middle of the night.

CU's coaches check the daily class attendance of freshmen and all other players whose grade point average is below 2.1. Those who miss class, like those who miss Breakfast Club, go to Commitment Time. So do those who miss the mandatory 8 a.m. study table for players who don't have class at that hour.

"Coach Barnett doesn't mess around," Hagan said, sounding a bit like Strother Martin himself. "If you miss breakfast, it's Commitment Time. If you show up for study table at 8:01, it's Commitment Time." Hagan should know. As a player he had once missed a class because of a knee injury. Then-coach Bill McCartney instructed Barnett, then the backfield coach, to punish the star quarterback. "He had me in the field house at 5 a.m.," Hagan recalled. "I couldn't run, but he made me walk around the filed house on crutches.

Barnett still remembers the incident.

"It was Darian and (then-fullback) George Hemingway," he said. "I was mad because I had to be out there at 5 o'clock with them."

While I was sitting in a film session with Barnett and defensive coordinator Mike Hankwitz after Breakfast Club, Hagan walked in and showed Barnett the clipboard. There were names on the Breakfast Club no-show list.

"Here they are," Hagan said.

"Get them out there running tomorrow morning," Barnett said as he looked at the clipboard. "It looks like we just got some more guys for Commitment Time, too."

Bye week was certainly not shaping up as off week. But it was the closest thing to a break the Colorado football team would get for a while. As the weather got colder, the rain would turn to snow. It would start getting dark early and the team would begin a march through more dark times—this time on the field.

Although they didn't yet know it, October was going to be a long month for the CU Buffaloes.

They were going to play five games in October and they were going to lose four of them.

Chapter Seven
On the Way Home

Given the partially self-induced public relations beating he had taken in his adopted home state over the previous eight grueling months, Gary Barnett was understandably happy to be returning to his home state to play his alma mater.

Barnett's trip to Missouri, however, would become less of a joyous homecoming when he and his players took the field to chants of "Rapists, Rapists," and left the field to even more verbal abuse by Missouri's fans.

When speaking publicly prior to his team's second road trip of the season, Barnett downplayed the personal importance of playing the University of Missouri. A 1969 graduate of the school, he lettered as a wide receiver there and continued his courtship of high-school sweetheart Mary Weil, who would become his wife before the two graduated.

But privately it was another matter.

"I don't need to tell you what this game means," he said at the Thursday night team meeting before telling them anyway.

"This is big-boy football," he boomed from the stage in the team auditorium before telling his young team about the increased intensity and game speed of a Big 12 game. The inexperienced team probably needed that speech. Six transfers in the wake of the scandalous allegations had combined with graduation and injuries to make his team even younger than Barnett had thought it would be. Going into the 2004 season, Ron Monteilh was the only wide receiver to have ever caught a pass in a college game. The most experienced players in the defensive secondary were sophomores and, through three games, that secondary had given up more yards than all but three teams in the nation.

But Barnett had history on his side. Both he and CU had seemed to own the Missouri Tigers over the past two decades. CU had a 17-2 record against the Tigers over the past 19 years and Barnett had a combined 11-1 record against them as an assistant or head coach. He was 5-0 against his old school as a head coach.

Even from a vantage point in the back row of the auditorium, it was apparent that this week was going to be different from the previous four. The trip was going to be more difficult both on and off the field. Barnett alerted his players to the hard landing they would make when the team charter landed at the Columbia airport. "It's a short field," he said. "We're going to hit down hard and there will be a screeching sound." Bad choice of words, I thought, thankful that I was taking a commercial flight to Kansas City and driving to Columbia. After the meeting, football operations director David Hansburg laughed about Barnett's dire airport warning.

"That's nothing," Hansburg said. "When I was at Idaho, our team plane landed on a short runway all the time. We used to hit so hard it made the oxygen bags drop down."

Near the end of the meeting Barnett told his team of that night's 11 p.m. curfew. The team bus would leave Boulder the next morning at 10:20 and the team plane would leave Denver at noon. The rest of the day was tightly scheduled, with a walk-through practice squeezed in between the landing in Columbia and the bus ride to the Holiday Inn that routinely housed the visiting teams. Dinner was to be wrapped around a series of meetings and the evening snack was scheduled for 9 p.m. Although wake-up call was not until 9 a.m., lights out was set for 10:45 p.m. The players, however, didn't miss much by going to bed early. It rained off-and-on through the night.

The Missouri trip was my last with Steve Hemphill, our newspaper's CU beat writer. Steve, with whom I had been friends for 10 years, was moving to a paper in Roanoke, Virginia, in a week. With the exception of Lincoln, Nebraska, I had never been to a Big 12 city and was counting on him for guidance. The first hint that we weren't in Denver or Boulder came at Kansas City International Airport, which appeared about as international as the International House of Pancakes. The rental car clerk bragged about the cool car she was getting us, a bright orange Ford Mustang with a hood scoop and a fancy stereo system.

There should have been a billboard saying: "Welcome to Middle America."

In a way, there was.

Along I-70 on the eastern edge of Kansas City sat two billboards that went a long way in explaining where we were. The one of the left side of the highway advertised the upcoming Billy Graham Crusade. The other billboard advertised a strip club.

We stopped for lunch on the eastern edge of Kansas City at a Gates barbecue restaurant, which I learned was one of the best barbecue places in the KC area. And KC was known for great barbecue.

The door hadn't hit us in the butt before a friendly counter clerk belted out what sounded like a one-word greeting.

"Himayihepya," she said.

"What did she say?" I asked.

"Hi, may I help you?" Hemphill responded. "They say that every time someone walks in the door. Let's get the sampler. You get pork, chicken AND brisket."

Gates had great food and nice people. They were definitely nicer than some I would later encounter in Columbia.

The scene got more interesting as we approached Columbia along the collection of fireworks stores and pornography super stores known to the rest of the world as Interstate 70. It suddenly became clear why the bar in the Columbia Holiday Inn was called "Spanky's."

When Barnett and the team arrived at the Holiday Inn, they had plenty of company. Several cars with CU flags, including a huge black SUV with Texas plates belonging to the parents of CU tackle Clint O'Neil, sat in the parking lot. Defensive coordinator Mike Hankwitz's brother, Terry, had driven from Michigan for the game.

The weekend was shaping up as somewhat of a Barnett family reunion. Both Mary and Gary Barnett had their mothers there. Their son Clay, who was in his last semester at the University of Denver Law School, was also there. Missing was Gary and Mary's recently-married daughter, Courtney, whose wedding reception had been held at the family home outside Boulder. Courtney had been out of the country most of the past few years, doing humanitarian health-education work in some pretty inhospitable places. She had watched the World Trade Center towers collapse on a TV set in Moscow and her work later took her to places such as Afghanistan.

While most of the Barnett family was in Columbia for the game, they probably couldn't have been more unwelcome. Since early in the week, Missouri fans on the Internet "Tigerboard" chat room had been letting Barnett and the Buffs have it. And the loathing went beyond the normal hate-filled banter exchanged between opposing chat-room fans before a big game, singling out accusations of rape and recruiting conducted through the proliferation of free alcohol and sex. The Missouri fans even blasted former CU coach Bill McCartney, who had retired 10 years before.

The longstanding series between Colorado and Missouri had never been confused with the Ohio State-Michigan rivalry, but the so-called scandal, along with numerous predictions that the talented Tigers would win their first-ever Big 12 North championship, had given the confident Missouri fans plenty of fodder to use on the team that had suddenly become a big rival.

"Goddamn cockroaches," one Missouri fan wrote. Fans of the school so nice they named it thrice—Missouri, Missour-ah and Mizzou—had long memories, and their chat board proved it. There were several references to the infamous "fifth down" game played in Columbia in 1990 in which CU won, 33-31, after the referees mistakenly gave Colorado an additional play that resulted in a game-winning touchdown. McCartney, who was CU's coach at the time and who is also a Missouri graduate, was still being vilified at Missouri. Other insults on the Missouri chat board included references to hookers and sex parties, two subjects that would continue to haunt CU on the road all year.

After the Friday-night team dinner and meetings, Barnett stopped in on a family gathering in the hotel restaurant. On my way back from a walk interrupted by rain I didn't see coming, I saw a tall, white-haired man smoking a cigarette outside the restaurant. I introduced myself.

"I'm Mike Barnett," the tall guy said. "I'm Gary Barnett's brother."

He sure didn't look like him. Although two years younger than his now-famous brother, he had already seen most of his hair turn white. And, unlike his older brother, he smoked.

"I'll bet he gives you a lot of heat about smoking," I told him, remembering the badgering Barnett routinely gave me on the same subject.

"Oh, yeah," he said.

Mike Barnett was involved in real estate and still lived in the tiny town of Mexico, Missouri, the town the Barnetts left for the St. Louis suburbs when Gary was a high school freshman. Gary Barnett later told me Mike was the best athlete in the family and certainly better than his over-achieving older brother, who managed to earn a football letter as a senior at Missouri. Gary Barnett, who graduated from Mizzou in 1969 after playing for legendary coach Dan Devine, got into coaching almost immediately after graduation. While earning his master's degree in education, he became a graduate assistant for Devine's successor, Al Onofrio, and married Mary Weil.

In the summer of 1971 the newly-married Barnetts moved to Colorado Springs, where they got jobs teaching in the suburban Air Academy School District. They also bought a lot for $5,000 and built a house on it for another $20,000. It was a dream home for the young couple who would soon have two young children.

Barnett spent his first two teaching years as the offensive coordinator at Air Academy High School, which sits only a stone's throw from the United States Air Force Academy in the foothills north of Colorado Springs. In 1973 he was named the head coach and revived a program that went on to win six conference titles in his nine years as head coach. His team reached the semifinals of the state playoffs in both 1980 and 1981, and in 1982 he got his first college head-coaching job at tiny Fort Lewis College in the southwestern Colorado town of Durango. Fort Lewis was the smallest school in small-school Rocky Mountain Athletic Conference and rarely enjoyed success. It didn't enjoy much more under Barnett, whose teams went 4-5-1 in 1982 and 4-6 in 1983. Barnett left to become an assistant under McCartney in 1984, the year his old players at Fort Lewis won the only conference title in the school's history.

That was more than CU would do in Barnett's first year as an assistant. The Buffaloes were 1-10 that year, a record that convinced McCartney to install the wishbone offense in an attempt to solidify the thin ice upon which his job was resting. Barnett coached the quarterbacks and the fullbacks in the wishbone, an offense in which passes are almost never thrown, and the switch paid off in 1985 when CU went 7-5 in a season that almost certainly saved McCartney's job. Barnett continued as the quarterback-fullback coach until December of 1990, when he was named offensive coordinator in the wake of Jerry DiNardo's exit to take the head coaching job at Vanderbilt.

Barnett assumed his new duties less than a month before the biggest game in the school's history, the 1990 Orange Bowl in which CU defeated Notre Dame 10-9 to claim a national championship.

The ambitious Barnett spent one more season, his eighth, as a CU assistant before being named the head coach at Northwestern, which had something in common with Fort Lewis College.

Opposing teams considered them both great homecoming opponents.

Barnett had his work cut out for him at the helm of the football program at the Big 10's smart-kid school, which competed against the likes of Michigan, Ohio State, Wisconsin and Purdue. His first three years at Northwestern produced results that must have made him feel like he was back at Fort Lewis—records of 3-8, 2-9 and 3-7-1. In 1995, however, his team went 10-1 in the regular season, losing only to Miami of Ohio and beating teams like Ohio State, Penn State, Iowa and Michigan to land Northwestern only its second-ever berth in the Rose Bowl. Barnett's Northwestern Wildcats won the big 10 again in 1996 with a 9-2 regular-season record before losing to Tennessee 48-28 in the Citrus Bowl. The next two years bring 5-7 and 3-9 records, but Barnett was still a hot coaching prospect.

But the boy from Mexico, Missouri, who enjoys watching Seinfeld reruns, was still a small-town square at heart. After being named the national coach of the year after the 1995 season, he refused to accept the award.

"I was honored, but the award was sponsored by Playboy," he said. "I didn't think that was appropriate." Years later in the summer of 1999, he was invited to attend a dinner in Los Angeles with offensive lineman Ryan Johanningeier, who had been chosen a pre-season All-American.

"It's sponsored by Playboy," he told reporters before declining the invitation. "My wife wouldn't let me back in the house if I went."

Even without awards from Playboy, Barnett was about to move up.

When Rick Neuheisel abruptly left Colorado to take the head coaching job at the University of Washington in January of 1999, speculation ran wild as to who would succeed him. Early on, CU officials approached Denver Broncos offensive coordinator Gary Kubiak, who decided he wasn't interested. Fans threw out the name of Dave Logan, a former CU and Cleveland Browns wide receiver who was a highly-successful high school coach in suburban Denver but who had never coached at the college level. Attention then turned to Barnett, who accepted the job and angered both the fans of Northwestern and the Chicago media. They saw him as a carpetbagger, but those close to Barnett knew Colorado was his dream job. Reporters told and re-told the story of how Mary and Gary Barnett, while driving into Boulder in 1999, stopped at the scenic overlook a couple miles south of Boulder and wept as they gazed down on one of America's most beautiful cities. They had no idea how ugly that picturesque city would become five years later.

The Barnetts may have arrived back in Colorado on Cloud Nine, but they would later learn that Neuheisel had left a dark cloud behind him. CU would end up self-reporting itself and Neuheisel to the NCAA for a series of minor violations that involved recruiting and which were apparently brought to light by coaches at Nebraska. In addition to having prohibited contact with recruits during the NCAA's "dead period," Neuheisel and his staff had apparently allowed the CU equipment room to become a trick-or-treat bag for visiting recruits.

On the night reporters gathered for a press conference to announce Neuheisel's departure, prized Houston-area linebacker recruit Cory Redding stood in the cold outside the Dal Ward Center. But he wasn't exactly cold. He was wearing a down CU parka "loaned" to him by the coaches. Redding, who seemed dazed to hear that Neuheisel was leaving on the very night he was supposed to be entertaining his most-prized recruits, left Boulder and later visited Nebraska, but ended up signing with Texas.

The parka left Boulder with him.

When he wore the coat to Lincoln the Nebraska coaches, who knew that schools were supposed to retrieve any clothing loaned to recruits during a visit, noticed.

Eventually, so did the NCAA.

An investigation was underway.

The sins of the Neuheisel administration would eventually be atoned for by the Barnett administration. CU was placed on probation for two years and lost five of the allowed 85 scholarships for the 2003 season. The equipment room at CU has since turned into the Fort Knox of college football. When recruits are given a tour of the room, an immediate inventory is taken to make sure there are no jerseys, jackets, gloves or socks missing. In spite of later allegations that he allowed the football program to run wild, it didn't take long for Barnett to establish himself as the disciplinarian that Neuheisel had never pretended to be. Barnett's hiring was lauded by alumni and fans who saw Neuheisel's teams as soft or weak. Besides, Barnett was a "CU guy." He had been on McCartney's staff during the national championship run and the period when the Buffs won three straight Big 8 championships. Fans believed that, unlike Neuheisel, Barnett understood and embraced the physical nature of Big 12 football.

It took only a few weeks at CU for Barnett to display the plain-spoken nature that would mark his tenure and which would nearly cost him his job five years later. Prior to his first spring practice, he criticized the team's weight program, publicly admitting that his players weren't as physically strong as he thought they would be. That opinion solidified support among boosters and former players who complained that the team had come to resemble what they called a "Pac-10" team, not the type of big, physical running team necessary to win in the Big 12. Without criticizing Neuheisel directly, Barnett expressed his belief that the team had slipped during the Neuheisel years by adopting the slogan "Return to Dominance." It appeared to be the slogan of a man either supremely confident or extremely foolhardy.

The Buffaloes finished Barnett's first season with a 7-5 record that included a 5-3 record and a third-place finish in the Big 12 North behind Nebraska and Kansas State. But his second season threatened to make a joke of his brash Return to Dominance theme. While operating with two true freshmen who the year before had been the state's top two recruits, quarterback Craig Ochs and tailback Marcus Houston, the team stumbled badly. An 0-3 non-conference record would get worse with a 44-21 home loss to Kansas State in the first Big 12 game of the year. A win at Texas A&M was followed by losses to Texas and Kansas. After winning their next two games against Oklahoma State and Missouri, the Buffs would fall to then-lowly Iowa State and suffered a two-point loss to Nebraska to produce a 3-8 season. To make maters worse, Barnet's team had lost to in-state rival Colorado State two years in a row. Neuheisel's teams, on the other hand, had beaten CSU during all four of his years as CU's coach. Returning to dominance seemed like a pipe dream.

But it wasn't.

Barnett's 2001 team would catch fire after a demoralizing 24-22 home loss to Fresno State in 90-degree heat. While the loss to Fresno would quickly be forgotten on the team's way to the Big 12 championship and an eventual Number 3 national ranking, Barnett's candid postgame comments, however, would haunt him during that season. When reporters asked about a late-game interception thrown by quarterback Craig Och's late-game interception at a point when a field goal would have won the game, Barnett said Ochs had made a mistake and shouldn't have thrown the pass. The comment privately rankled Ochs and his family and Barnett was censured in the media for publicly criticizing a player. Injuries would later bench Ochs and Houston, Barnett's prize recruits, and both would later leave the program. But the emergence of transfer running back Chris Brown and sophomore tailback Bobby Purify, coupled with the play of transfer quarterback Bobby Pesavanto, would obscure the simmering feud of 2001. A 62-36 home win over Nebraska would ignite the kind of excitement that produced T-shirts emblazoned with the score and a 39-37 win over Texas would earn the Buffs their first Big 12 championship since the McCartney years.

While November of 2001 brought celebration to the Dal Ward Center, December would bring the ill-fated party at Lisa Simpson's apartment. January 1 would bring a disappointing effort in a 38-16 loss to Oregon in the Fiesta Bowl, but, in spite of that bowl loss, most CU fans were convinced the program had returned to dominance in 2001.

With both Ochs and Houston hobbled by injuries, CU had its work cut out for it in 2002. Operating behind unheralded junior-college transfer quarterback Robert Hodge and an offensive line that helped Brown run for 1,744 yards and Purify for 739, the team surprised many with a 9-5 record and its second-straight Big 12 North crown. The season ended on two down notes, however, with a 29-7 loss to Oklahoma in the Big 12 Championship game and a 31-28 loss to Wisconsin in the Alamo Bowl.

In 2003 both Ochs and Houston transferred and the team that had seemed poised to dominate was forced to rebuild. Ochs, who has suffered several concussions and who had to-this-day unexplained differences with the CU coaches, transferred to Montana while claiming Barnett once interrupted him during an on-field prayer after practice. Joel Klatt, the quarterback who started for CU in both 2003 and 2004, is also very religious and often joins his teammates in on-field prayer, but he has had no run-ins with Barnett on that subject. Houston, who had watched himself slip to number three on the depth chart behind Brown and Purify, transferred to Colorado State after alleging that running-backs coach Eric Bienemy had questioned his manhood and called him "Markeesha," a girl's name. Brown, meanwhile, left at the end of his junior year to enter the NFL draft. Purify, who had been heralded as Brown's replacement, suffered a high ankle sprain and missed all but three games. He was replaced by freshman Brian Calhoun, who the next year transferred to Wisconsin in the wake of the "recruiting scandal." Klatt, then a 20-year-old former minor-league baseball player, walked on and became the team's starting quarterback. The team lost to Colorado State for the fourth time in Barnett's five seasons and finished with a 5-7 record, but the team's problems paled in comparison to the problems it would face in the months following that season. 2004 would bring the now infamous "recruiting scandal."

It would also bring Barnett's ill-fated "terrible kicker" comments regarding Katie Hnida. His brutal honesty bought him a three-month suspension and tarnished a reputation he had taken decades to build. During his winter of discontent, Barnett spent time playing golf at his vacation home near Phoenix. Through the agency that represented him, he signed up for a course in media relations that he hoped would teach him how much to say and when to say it.

That course apparently served him well. While on suspension he carefully chose his media opportunities and agreed to tape an interview with Bernard Goldberg for HBO's "Inside Sports."

Goldberg, who had been pushed out after a long career at CBS News, was himself a vocal critic of what he believed to be a biased media. He had written a scathing book called "Bias," in which he ripped both CBS and anchor Dan Rather, whose own career would be tainted later in the year when the network broadcast stories based on supposedly-genuine documents indicating that President George Bush had shirked his duty while a member of the Air National Guard during the Vietnam era. While Goldberg and Barnett had a lot to agree on, Goldberg didn't give him much of a break in the interview. He asked hard questions and pushed Barnett for answers. The interview gave Barnett a chance to tell his side as well as the opportunity to admit he shouldn't have made the comments about Hnida. His media savvy seemed to have improved and, in subsequent interviews, he appeared to choose his words more carefully. He was getting better at this media business, but had paid a heavy price for his education.

Minutes before his team took the field for its game at Missouri, Barnett continued to issue warnings to his players, most of whom had never played in Columbia. Hundreds of cars with tiger tails sticking from their trunks were still heading to the parking lots when he told the team, "They're pretty chirpy out there. Just do your job and don't respond to them." That wasn't the first time he had admonished the team about playing at Faurot Field.

"There are going to be 65,000-plus in the stadium," he has said during his Thursday-night speech. "And, you've got the students right behind you. There will be a lot of heckling."

Barnett's prediction came true.

"No means no," fans shouted as the team formed up outside the locker room just before kickoff.

"Where the hookers at?" one man screamed.

Those who had begun the crusade against the football program in Boulder were seeing the fruits of their labors. District

Attorney Mary Keenan's allegations that Barnett had used alcohol and sex to attract recruits had found willing ears across the country.

As the CU players waited for the pre-game festivities to end, several hundred motorcycles pulled up at the south end of the stadium as they prepared to circle the field. The noise from a couple hundred Harley-Davidson's was deafening, but it seemed to get the CU players pumped up. Matt McChesney, a self-confessed Harley lover, jumped up and down and waved his arms as the engines roared. On the sideline an overweight Missouri fan was hurrying to finish painting the "I" in Missouri on his large stomach.

As the team ran out under the south stands, a liquid one could only hope was water or beer poured out of the stands. Clay Barnett, who had seen a lot growing up in a football family, seemed to take the abuse in stride.

"This really makes me miss football," he said. Three hours later the coach's son was probably glad he was pursuing an occupation different from that of his father.

Missouri started the game looking very much like the team picked to win the Big 12 North. The Tigers went 80 yards on 12 plays and tailback Damien Nash scored from the 3-yard line to put his team up 7-0. CU, looking very much like the team that had squeaked by Colorado State and Washington State, had its first possession snuffed by an interception on its third play. The Buffs managed a 37-yard Mason Crosby field goal on their second possession to cut Missouri's lead to four points, but Mizzou got a 53-yard field goal from Joe Tantarelli on the next series to go up 10-3. CU would get its second and last score of the game on the next series. On a drive that began with a 32-yard run by Purify, the Buffs would get their only touchdown of the game when Purify scored on a 4-yard run. The extra point attempt was blocked, but CU was within a point at 10-9.

That score didn't last very deep into the third quarter. CU was forced to punt after three plays and four plays later Missouri quarterback Brad Smith threw a 51-yard touchdown to Sean Coffey to give MU a 17-9 lead. CU quarterback Joel Klatt threw an interception on CU's next possession, but the Tigers let the buffs off the hook when Tantarelli missed a 42-yard field goal. Minutes later Tantarelli missed a 39-yard field goal and early in the fourth quarter CU had a chance to tie the game. On a second-and-goal play from the Missouri 7, Klatt threw what appeared to be a touchdown pass to Evan Judge, but Missouri defensive back Shird Mitchell stole the ball away as the two were coming down.

"It looked as though he caught it and it was stolen out of his arms,' ABC color commentator Terry Bowden said of the play. The referees, however, ruled that Mitchell had taken the ball away before Judge's foot hit the ground. It would be CU's last scoring chance of the day. As time ticked away for the Buffs, Bowden praised the way the CU team had responded to "all the stuff in the off season." Now it was the current season that was threatening to tick away.

Barnett had lost to Missouri for the first time in his head coaching career.

CU had gained 13 first downs, while Missouri racked up 22.

Purify, who injured his left shoulder in the game, had been held to 80 yards, while Missouri's backs rolled up 228 rushing yards.

Missouri had also controlled the ball for nearly 10 minutes longer than CU.

Had Tantarelli not missed three field goals, the damage would have been worse. There was plenty of blame to spread around.

For the first time in the 2004 season, the players didn't get to sing their victorious fight song after the game.

"We all made too many mistakes to win this game," Barnett said in the quiet locker room. "Coaches, players, we all made too many mistakes. We have to keep believing in each other."

That belief would be tested throughout October. Missouri, meanwhile, would win its next game against Baylor before dropping five in a row. Ironically, the Buffs would find themselves rooting for Missouri on the last weekend of the season as part of a complicated scenario that would decide the Big 12 North title.

As the CU players grabbed pizzas from a giant rack inside the locker room and headed for the bus just outside, Missouri fans leaned over the concrete walls above the locker room. The insults continued and the gloating had begun, but the mothers of both Mary and Gary Barnett missed all of that. They were lucky. They had watched the game from the team hotel.

The team plane landed at Denver International Airport just before 9 o'clock that night. Unlike the landing in Columbia, there was no loud thud and no screeching noise when the plane landed.

In coming weeks, however, CU's 2004 season would come close to crash landing.

And the ongoing scandal would provide plenty of screeching.

Chapter Eight
She Hate Me

Preparation, it is said in football, is everything.

As they stared out the windows of the team bus on the ride from the airport to Boulder after their loss at Missouri, CU's players were already thinking about preparations for their next two successive home games. Their 3-1 record, however, somehow seemed more like 1-3 and hadn't generated any excitement from fans frustrated by the team's offensive woes. While talk of the scandal had subsided somewhat on the radio talk shows, it had been replaced with talk of how CU couldn't generate an offense. CU's coaches, meanwhile, were trying to recruit new players in the face of the scandal allegations.

A lot had gone wrong in the Missouri game and the fixes would have to come fast.

The next two weeks would bring home games against highly-touted Oklahoma State and Iowa State, which was about to make a surprising run at the Big 12 North title. Preparations for those teams were routine. Coaches, as they always did, spent Sunday morning looking at films of both their team and Oklahoma State's. Preparing for the Cowboys was routine.

But there was nothing routine about—and no way the CU football program could have prepared for—the opponent it had been fighting for most of 2004. That opponent was one with no game film to study, but one with a game plan that would continue to threaten the football program. That team, CU learned the hard way, didn't have to follow any rules. It made the rules. It had been beating CU senseless in the court of public opinion.

Supporters of CU had derisively referred to that team, which included several lawyers and a press agent, as Team Simpson.

My research told me it could just have well been called Team Keenan.

While CU coach Gary Barnett has routinely offered only a "no comment" when asked about Boulder DA Mary Keenan and her perceived role in the scandalous charges leveled at his program, in early 2004 he acknowledged that the program's opponents were well prepared and had "scouted" the CU program well.

"I've felt all along that it's been orchestrated by someone who knows our weaknesses and knew what our limitations are in our ability to defend ourselves," he said in an assessment that could well have applied to an upcoming on-field opponent. He was right. He and his program were facing a formidable opponent who came into battle much more prepared than the state's largest university.

When CU student Lisa Simpson filed a sexual-harassment suit against the university in late 2002, she was represented by Boulder attorney Baine Kerr. Later she would have her own press agent, Lisa Simon of Denver-based Prescient Communications. She was also encouraged by the words of Boulder District Attorney Mary Keenan, who, after failing to file rape charges connected with Simpson's claim that she was raped by CU football players and recruits at a December, 2001 party, advised Simpson of her right to sue in civil court. In fact, it was Keenan's deposition, in which she claimed CU used sex and alcohol to attract recruits, that brought the "CU scandal" national media attention.

Team Simpson was also blessed with close ties to a member of the University of Colorado Board of Regents, a member who just happens to be married to Simpson's lawyer.

While admitting that she met several times with Simpson's attorneys, including a meeting in they asked her to file criminal perjury charges against CU officials they believed had lied in their depositions, Keenan continues to claim she did nothing wrong.

"I've treated both sides the same way," she told me in February of 2004, "with courtesy."

The players who were not charged with rape by Keenan but who became the target of her public assertion that sex and alcohol were used to recruit would certainly differ with that. They could argue that the DA's public assertion that she believed the rapes occurred but were not prosecuted because of identity problems is not the most courteous of treatment, especially when those allegations cast a cloud over dozens of innocent young men and the coaches.

Inexplicably, the media failed to question the involvement Keenan may have had in the Simpson case and failed to question if that was appropriate behavior for the DA's office. They also turned a blind eye to what some reporters considered her long-standing practice of bullying and manipulating them. It is a record that, according to reporters willing to talk about it, includes efforts to keep the arrests of her own adult children out of the news and her attempt to keep quiet the drunk-driving arrest of one of her top deputy prosecutors.

Keenan has been a very outspoken critic of CU coach Gary Barnett and has accused him of failing to keep a close enough eye on his football family. As I covered the ever-growing story of the CU scandal throughout 2004, it became increasingly frustrating to watch the media's failure to report the conduct of anyone except the football players. While Gary Barnett and his football family have become fair game for negative press, Keenan has tried to make sure her own family avoids such publicity, especially when that publicity involved trouble with the law.

Travis Henry, a former colleague of mine at the *Longmont Daily Times-Call* and one of the brightest, toughest journalists in Colorado, covered Keenan's office for several years and remembers several instances in which she tried to keep arrests out of print. One of those efforts actually worked, albeit briefly. It was Henry who stymied her efforts in that case.

On November 24, 2001 a Boulder police officer pulled over Keenan's 31-year-old daughter, Tavis, allegedly because she was driving erratically. Police reports said Keenan's daughter struck a utility pole before backing into the police car while she was pulling over. She was cited for driving under the influence and careless driving. The *Longmont Times-Call* reporter who was filling in for the vacationing Henry and who had previously displayed a soft spot for Keenan because of her reputation for aggressive prosecution of sex offenders, didn't think the story was newsworthy. That reporter's bias was quickly uncovered and corrected. Upon his return Henry noticed the police report at the Boulder County Justice Center and asked his colleagues why it hadn't been in the paper. His replacement said she didn't think the story was newsworthy. Her bosses disagreed and she was ordered to write the story. She did so, but refused to put her byline on the story.

Because of her mother's position as the county's chief prosecutor, a special prosecutor was appointed to hear Tavis Keenan's case. County Court Judge John Stavely, however, stayed on the case. He later approved a plea agreement under which Tavis Keenan pleaded guilty to the lesser offense of driving while impaired. Charges of driving-while-intoxicated and careless driving were dropped and Stavely sentenced her to two years of probation, alcohol treatment and 24 hours of community service. He suspended a 20-day jail sentence.

Henry also claimed that Keenan asked him to kill a story when one of her deputies, Ingrid Bakke, was arrested for driving while impaired by alcohol. Henry said that after he was promoted to the position of assistant city editor, Keenan called him and asked "if we could keep Ingrid Bakke's arrest out of the papers."

According to Henry, Keenan "made excuses" for her deputy, telling him that Bakke had been depressed about her mother's serious illness and that her blood-alcohol level at the time of her arrest was barely above the legal limit.

"I told her no," Henry said. The story ran.

Years later Bakke was "loaned out" to Eagle County prosecutors to assist in the prosecution of basketball star Kobe Bryant, who was charged with raping a hotel employee. Whispers in the legal community and critical public statements from the presiding judge intimated that the prosecution had done a sloppy job that included the non-timely filing of routine motions. The consensus was that they had been manhandled by Bryant's high-priced attorneys. And Bakke was considered the pride of Keenan' office.

In another incident, Henry said, Keenan asked him to kill a story in which a young woman accused her son, Brian, of striking her after she appeared at his home in the aftermath of their breakup. Henry said the woman, 25-year-old Robin Brower, appeared to be battered and bruised in photographs taken by police. According to Henry, Brower initially refused to tell the Boulder Community Hospital staff who injured her. "She told them, 'You wouldn't believe me if I told you,'" Henry said. "After they asked her several times, she told them it was Brian Keenan, the DA's son." Officials at the Boulder County Safe House also believed her. So did the police, until they went to Brian Keenan's home and interviewed him. Keenan's son insisted that Brower, who was drunk, broke into his house after breaking a window. He claimed she was injured when she fell down as he was "escorting her" out of the house.

"They believed her at first," Henry said, "but they changed their mind after talking to Brian Keenan. But they didn't even investigate it. That's the scary thing."

Brower, who admitted being drunk at the time of the incident, sustained a concussion and a cut to her elbow that required stitches. She claimed she sustained the injuries, which were photographed at the hospital, when Brian Keenan assaulted her. But getting police to believe the DA's son had assaulted her was not Brower's biggest legal problem. At the time of the incident, she was on probation for a marijuana charge. She was charged with felony mischief in connection with the broken windows and a conviction would result in revocation of her probation and almost certainly a prison term.

Brower agreed to plead no contest to a misdemeanor mischief charge in exchange for dismissal of the felony charge. Brian Keenan was never charged. At her sentencing hearing Brower broke down in tears. Her attorney, Megan Ring, told the judge her client had mixed emotions about the deal.

"Her position is her actions in breaking the windows were in self defense," Henry's story quoted Ring. Henry, who had covered dozens of domestic-violence cases in Boulder County, said the case was one of a kind.

"I don't know if the woman was telling the truth," he said, "but in every case I've seen where a girl came in beaten up in a domestic incident, they went after the guy. Not this time."

It was Mary Keenan who contacted Henry and asked him to leave her son's name out of the paper.

"She told me Brian had a tough year, a friend of his had recently died and that it would be unfair to put him in the story because he wasn't charged," Henry said. Keenan had no problem with the fairness of soiling the reputations of uncharged CU coaches and players when she, in a sworn deposition, said she believed alcohol and sex were being used to attract recruits and that she believed Lisa Simpson had been raped by either football players or recruits. She tolerated bad publicity when it affected those she did not like, but not when it affected her employees or family members.

According to Henry, that's not the only time Keenan tried to keep her son's name out of the paper. He said she made a similar request when that son was arrested for drunk driving in late 2000. Brian Keenan's DUI case raised even more eyebrows when a visiting judge, who replaced a Keenan friend in hearing the case, dismissed the charges. Visiting Judge David Ramirez granted a defense motion to throw the case out after Brian Keenan's lawyers argued that the officer who claimed he pulled Keenan's son over because he had no license-plate light had no probable cause to stop him. Ramirez ruled that since the officer was less than 50 feet from the back of the car, he didn't need to see the light to read the plate. Ramirez took the unusual step of noting that he was not setting a precedent with the ruling and that it only applied in that case.

Keenan's family-control problems went beyond that. Henry found that out early, thanks to a physical threat that Keenan laughed off.

According to Henry, Brian Keenan and three friends were among those who attended Mary Keenan's election-night victory celebration at the Red Fish restaurant in Boulder. Brian's three friends, Henry said, were "visibly drunk – eyes glazed over, trashed." At one point, Henry said, the three recognized him as a reporter and approached him.

"They told me if I wrote anything bad about Mary they would kick my ass," he said, adding that he approached the DA and told her of the threat. She dismissed it out of hand.

"She said they were just kidding,' Henry said. "They weren't kidding. If I hadn't been on the job and sober, I would have fought them. I guess they didn't push me quite far enough."

When Henry told me that story I wondered what Keenan would have done if three CU football players had made a public threat to injure someone. Certainly Mary Keenan is not responsible for the conduct of her adult children, but her repeated attempts to manipulate the media certainly can give a reasonable person cause to pause. I found that out myself in February of 2004 when she warned me not to write negative things about her and said she "gets mean when I'm pissed off."

More disturbing than Keenan's actions, however, is the free pass she has gotten from reporters over the years. Newspapers don't run articles that say "DA Tries To Keep Names Out" or "DA's Drunken Thugs Threaten Reporter."

In addition to serving as something of a publicity machine for the Simpson-Gilmore claims, Keenan is likely to serve a much more critical role in the suit if it is revived by the appellate court—the suit, let's remember, that a judge threw out of court. Several prominent employment lawyers told me that in order to win a sexual-harassment claim under the federal Title IX law guaranteeing equal access to employment opportunities, plaintiffs must show that the offending party, in this case CU, was informed of the problem and subsequently did virtually nothing to correct it. Lawyers for Simpson and Gilmore have argued in their appeals that new evidence will show CU was fully aware of the problems and chose to ignore them, while CU lawyers have said the appeal is merely a rehash of issues earlier decided by a judge.

Keenan is the central figure in the argument that CU knew of sexual harassment and rape prior to the 2001 party. In her now-famous deposition, she claimed CU was "put on notice" in early 1998 during a meeting with then-athletic director Dick Tharp, Chancellor Richard Byyny and senior associate athletic director Bob Chichester. The meeting was called after a December 1997 incident at Boulder's Harvest House Hotel in which a 17-year-old high school student claimed to have been raped. That party, held under the watch of former coach Rick Neuheisel, was reportedly attended by both CU players and recruits. Like the December 2001 party, it did not result in the filing of sex-assault charges. Keenan said she acted as the "heavy" in that meeting, but her boss at the time, former DA Alex Hunter, remembered the meeting much differently.

Hunter, in a deposition taken in the Simpson case, said it would be "an extraordinary exaggeration" to say his office believed CU was using alcohol and sex to attract recruits. "We did have concerns that the university was not paying enough attention," Hunter said in his deposition, adding he "had an expectation" that CU would put tighter reigns on its recruiting process. Barnett, of course, didn't work at CU at the time and wasn't hired until a year after the meeting. Keenan, however, said he knew of the 1997 incident. She said that when Barnett was hired she asked her friend and former roommate Anne Ankney, who was then Barnett's secretary, to convey the message. Ankney told Keenan she delivered the message, but later admitted she lied about telling Keenan.

"I thought about it several times and I could never find the proper time, and I never felt comfortable about bringing it up," Ankney said in her own deposition. While Keenan at the time depended on a friend to relay such an important message to Barnett, she later said it didn't matter that Ankney lied to her and didn't pass the information on to Barnett.

In June of 2004 Keenan told Lyn Bartels of the *Rocky Mountain News* that it didn't matter if Ankney was lying and it didn't matter if Ankney failed to relay the messages because Keenan told Barnett's bosses of the problems.

Chichester, who no longer works for CU, agreed with Keenan's story and said he discussed the problem with Barnett. In his deposition Barnett said he wasn't told of the 1997 Harvest House incident by Chichester, Tharp or anyone else until the 2001 incident. Chichester, in his deposition, called Keenan "a close friend of mine," and said he told both Byyny and Tharp that the DA's office believed "opportunities were being provided for the recruits to have sex with women."

Former CU regent Bob Sievers, who served 12 years on the university's governing board, said fellow-Democrat Keenan never mentioned problems at CU while he was in office.

"We campaigned together, we were in social settings," Sievers said, "and she never raised any concerns with me, in spite of the fact that I was on the board of regents. She had many opportunities to bring it up to me, but never did."

Keenan isn't the only figure in the case with a record of manipulating the media, according to Henry. Simpson attorney Baine Kerr, he said, has a similar track record.

"He was the master of calling (reporters) and publicizing his cases," Henry said. "That's how I knew him. He was trying to manipulate the media long before the Simpson case." He said Kerr also wasn't shy about calling the media when he didn't like a story. "He would call and yell if we wrote anything he didn't like," Henry said.

I can certainly vouch for that.

When I wrote a piece that detailed Kerr's hiring of Prescient Communications to aid the Simpson case and which gave details about Simpson's deposition and diary he didn't want published, he called me, too. Apparently under the assumption that I had failed ninth grade civics, he told me, "You are in violation of two federal court orders," knowing full well that the media was not under the gag order placed upon the parties in the case.

When it comes to manipulating the media, Kerr seemed to want it both ways. While he is free to try his cases in the newspapers, others apparently are not. In 2004 he filed a grievance with the Colorado Supreme Court claiming that Barnett's attorney, John Rodman, had acted inappropriately by taking calls from the media during the coach's suspension. The Colorado Supreme Court Discipline Committee found the grievance to be without merit. It's hard to fathom how a lawyer who hires a publicist for a case and who reaches out to the media can criticize anyone else, but it happened.

And the media ignored it.

Reporters have been similarly kind to CU Regent Cindy Carlisle, who defeated Sievers by a 2-1 margin the 2002 Democratic Primary Election and who is married to Kerr. To its credit, the *Boulder Daily Camera* addressed Carlisle's potential conflict of interest in a February 2004 article announcing a regent meeting called to discuss the football allegations. In the article Carlisle said she would "recuse" herself from discussing the lawsuit being litigated by her husband, but the same article also quoted CU Alumni Association member Michael Kennedy as saying the recusal would not be enough and that she should resign her post.

Carlisle scoffed at that notion, saying Kennedy was dead wrong and that she had a duty to serve her term. Within days Carlisle voted against the appointment of Joyce Lawrence and Peggy Lamm as co-chairs of the Independent Investigating Committee formed to investigate allegations of sexual wrongdoing in the football program. Carlisle, the regent who promised to stay out of the process that involved her husband, voted against Lamm and Lawrence because, according to the *Daily Camera* story, they lacked knowledge of acquaintance rape and other forms of violence against women and because they lacked legal backgrounds. Carlisle, who also alleged that Lawrence had demeaned the alleged female victims of the December 7 party that was at the crux of her husband's lawsuits, was criticized by some CU fans and player parents for taking part in that vote, but not by the media. Soon after that she announced she would not participate in the selection of the committee to avoid muddying the waters of the now-cross-pollinated investigation.

Those waters, however, were already muddied by her footprints. The investigative committee and her husband's lawsuit against the university were both rooted in the December, 2001 party. The two were inseparable, except to Carlisle, whose position as a regent afforded her a ringside seat to events that had everything to do with her husband's suit. The firing of former CU strength coach E.J. "Doc" Kreiss was a good example. Kreiss was fired in April of 2003 after allegations that he gave players who had run afoul of the law credit for community service hours while they were lifting weights. Barnett said that under state personnel laws he was prohibited from discussing the reasons for Kreiss' firing, but said, "When we learn of a violation, we address it immediately."

The firing of Kreiss was reportedly discussed by the regents in a closed executive session in May of 2003 and when I contacted Carlisle in February 2004 to ask her if she should have attended that session in light of her husband's suit, she used the state personnel law to avoid an answer.

"By law I can't respond to that at all," she said, "even to the extent of confirming that anything was discussed. I respect the executive session completely." Kerr, on the other hand, told me the details of Kreiss' activities were "non-confidential pubic information (received) from a Doc Kreiss supporter."

There was and is no way for the public to ensure that the line between lawyer Kerr and regent Carlisle is not erased. For the most part, reporters have let them off the hook. While the media has been kind to Carlisle regarding her potential conflict of interest, *Denver Post* reporter Jim Hughes was downright magnanimous. In a November 20, 2004 story carrying the headline "Regent wants to up ethics standard" he quoted Carlisle as saying fellow regent Jerry Rutledge should have disclosed the fact that Gary Barnett had purchased $10,000 worth of gift certificates for his assistants at Rutledge's clothing store. Carlisle intimated that the relationship between Barnett and Rutledge might appear to be improper. In that story Hughes failed to mention that Carlisle is married to the lawyer whose suit sparked both the "scandal" and every investigation that followed. He failed to ask her if she thought she had a conflict of interest. His bias was transparent, but apparently not to his editors at the *Post*. Didn't the reader, in the context of a conflict-of-interest story, have the right to know that the person being quoted had perhaps the largest appearance of impropriety issue of any of the regents?

Shortly after the board of regents defended Professor Ward Churchill's right to free speech in the wake of an inflammatory essay in which he compared the World Trade Center terror victims to Nazis, Carlisle found some speech that was apparently even more odious than Churchill's and decided to quash it. When I agreed to an interview with the *Buffalo Sports News*, a web-based college sports publication that covers CU, the organization's Web site advertised the interview. When he became aware of the interview CU's sports information director David Plati e-mailed the athletic staff an "FYI" message alerting them to the story. He made no suggestion that they read it and did not comment on its contents, but that didn't matter to Carlisle. A source told me she phoned the athletic department and informed them that it was "actionable" for Plati to alert the staff to "that kind of stuff."

So much for free speech.

When I learned that the regent who has sworn to remain on the sidelines of the lawsuit debate had put herself back in the game, I decided to find out why. I sent her the following e-mail.

Regent Carlisle:

It has come to my attention that you recently contacted CU officials and warned them that it is "actionable" for them to inform their colleagues about an interview with me on the BSN Web site. I have several questions for you as I complete work on my book about the CU scandal.

1. What prompted you to contact CU athletic officials regarding this matter? Do you believe they have the same freedom of speech and thought as you and the board of regents have afforded Professor Ward Churchill?

2. What did you mean by "actionable" and what action do you plan to take?

3. Do you believe you have a conflict of interest regarding the scandal, given the fact that your family stands to directly benefit financially from the Simpson-Gilmore suit?

4. As a regent, you have the legal right to read the grand jury report. Did you do so? If so, did you share its contents with your husband, Baine Kerr?

5. During the Independent Investigation Commission period, did you have any contact with commission member Peggy Lamm? This contact includes phone calls to and from your office or home and to and from her home and commission-supplied cell phone.

6. In your warning to athletic department officials you cautioned them against telling others about my interview, which you termed "that kind of stuff." What did you mean by "that kind of stuff?"

I appreciate and anticipate your prompt answers to my questions.
Respectfully, Bruce J. Plasket.

I would still like to know if she read any part of the grand jury report that her husband could have used to his advantage in the Simpson lawsuit and would still like to know the nature of her relationship with members of the investigative committee. I'm not holding my breath, however. Cindy Carlisle has yet to respond to my questions. The dismissal of her husband's lawsuit against the university she supposedly serves must have been quite an embarrassment for her. It would be even more embarrassing for her if reporters connected the dots between Carlisle and others who have vocally accused the football program of wrongdoing. Regina Cowles, the director of the Boulder chapter of the National Organization for Women who has publicly blasted the program at every opportunity, served as Carlisle's campaign manager during her 2002 run for the board of regents. That election was held almost exactly a month before Carlisle's husband filed the Simpson suit, but not one reporter has pointed out the possibility of a connection between Cowles, Carlisle and Kerr. Sievers, meanwhile, laughs at Carlisle's contention that she has no conflict of interest.

"She has an enormous conflict of interest," he said. "Everyone in the state thinks it's a conflict except her."

The football team, however, was thinking only about conflicts on the field as it prepared for Oklahoma State. Before the game I was secretly hoping CU would turn its season around and show those people a thing or two. Like the players, I was now hoping on-the-field success would convince the detractors that these young men were not, as I was discovering, the out-of-control thugs they had been portrayed as by Team Simpson. My affection for the players, however, did not cloud my belief that they would have their hands full with Oklahoma State, especially the way the offense had played in three of its first four games. I wasn't the only one with concerns about the offense. Internet chat-board fans possessing about as much football knowledge as I do were calling for fixes that included the benching of quarterback Joel Klatt and even the firing of offensive coordinator Shawn Watson. Those voices would get louder after the Oklahoma State game.

While playing in the shadow of Big 12 South giants Oklahoma and Texas, the Oklahoma State Cowboys came to

Boulder intent on backing up their Number 22 ranking in the polls. They did a great job. Running back Vernand Morency gave his team a 7-0 lead early in the first quarter with a 58-yard touchdown run and scored again five minutes later on a 6-yard run after a CU turnover. The Cowboys made it 21-0 on the last play of the first half when Donovan Woods threw a 58-yard touchdown pass to Elliot Prentiss. The CU locker room was glum at halftime, but the mood grew even darker before the day was done.

After battling OSU to a near-standstill for most of the third quarter, the CU defense gave up its 28th point of the day when Woods hit Luke Frazier for a 20-yard touchdown pass. CU responded with a 6-yard touchdown run by Lawrence Vickers early in the fourth quarter, but the Cowboys came right back with another long touchdown pass that put them up by a score of 35-7. Late in the fourth quarter Barnett replaced Klatt with James Cox, who threw a 21-yard touchdown pass to Dusty Sprague, but a subsequent touchdown on an interception return gave Oklahoma State a 42-14 win. Things that had gone wrong at Missouri had gotten only worse at home against Oklahoma State and the Buffs found themselves 0-2 in the Big 12 North.

Inside the sullen CU locker room Barnett, who after the Missouri loss admonished his team to "keep believing in each other," said many of the same things he had said the week before. Too many mistakes against a bad team, we need to fix what's wrong, he echoed. In his post-game press conference he called the game "an embarrassing performance for the team, players and the coaches." He vowed to "go in and look over things we did good" and once again vowed to "fix the things we did wrong." He also tried to deflect most of the blame onto himself. "We just fell victim to some mistakes and bad calls by the coach and questionable calls by the coach," he said. There were a lot of things that needed to be fixed before the Iowa State game.

Predictably, the game itinerary for the Iowa State game carried the words, "We Have Fixed It," followed by the phrase "Glad To Be Here." It was apparent he was fearful his players were going to give up on one another.

Changes were in order for the suddenly 3-2 Buffs. Little was made of safety Tom Hubbard's promotion to a starting position, but a lot was made of the announcement that sophomore James Cox would start at quarterback in place of Joel Klatt. Fans on the chat board hailed the change, while Cox and Klatt said all the right things about the decision being out of their hands. Cox, however, didn't seem nervous on the eve of his first collegiate start. Chewing on pizza as he sat in the lobby of the team hotel with his mother, aunt and younger brother, he yawned and seemed calm. "I'm tired. I'm going to bed," he announced to them as he headed upstairs an hour before the mandatory lights out.

Cox didn't appear any more nervous the next day as he prepared for his first college start. He calmly answered all of offensive coordinator Shawn Watson's questions as the offense went through a quiz on a scripted list of its first 15 plays in a pre-game meeting. On CU's first possession of the game he directed the team down the field and threw a 3-yard touchdown pass to tight end Jesse Wallace. But the day would belong to sophomore kicker Mason Crosby, who was born in Colorado but who had grown up in Georgetown, Texas. Crosby gave the Buffs a 10-0 lead with a 28-yard field goal mid-way through the first quarter and would extend the lead to 13-0 with 5:43 left in the second quarter with a 60-yard field goal that would break a 23-year-old school record. But, with 1:22 left in the second quarter Iowa State would get back in the game when Ellis Hobbs sneaked in front of an "out" route by a wide receiver and picked off a Cox pass, returning it for a touchdown that made the score 13-7. Crosby came to the rescue again on the last play of the first half when he kicked a 54-yard field goal and became the first college player to ever kick two 50-plus yard field goals in the same game.

Klatt started the second half at quarterback and heard scattered boos from fans who wanted to see more of Cox. Both Cox and Klatt would later downplay the quarterback switch and both would invoke the "team first' mantra. Both seemed to actually mean it. But it was still Crosby's day. He kicked his third field goal of the day, a 33-yarder, mid-way through the fourth quarter. Iowa State scored a late touchdown, but the Buffs had stopped their two-game skid with a 19-14 win.

"It was a win and we are 4-2," a relieved Barnett told reporters after the game while refusing to go into detail on the quarterback switch. Some reporters later reported that the CU coaching staff only intended for Cox to pay a half so that Klatt could get a break and a better view of the offense before going back in. Barnett was terse when asked about the decision to replace Cox with Klatt at the beginning of the second half. And he made it known it was his decision.

"I just said, 'We're playing Joel,'" he said. "I wanted experience in the game."

The Buffs had fixed just enough of their problems to win the game. But they would take a Big 12 North win any way they could get it. They had come through in their first do-or-die game of the season. As they would find out the next week at Texas A&M, those do-or-die games would soon become a weekly thing.

Even though the Simpson-Gilmore case has been dismissed, it still lingers in the courts and in the minds of the public as Barnett awaits a future that lies in the hands of new university president Hank Brown and new athletic director Mike Bohn. While Barnett and his advisors push for a contract extension he calls critical to recruiting, that future is anything but secure.

Barnett's contract says that "Only violations by student athletes, assistant coaches and/or university employees which (Barnett) had knowledge of or should have reasonably had knowledge of will be deemed 'just cause for termination.'"

So far no one has tied Barnett to the handful of indiscretions committed by the handful of players he subsequently disciplined for their actions, but the atmosphere created by Keenan and Kerr and fostered by the media would make preparations for the future nearly impossible.

During the team's trip to Texas A&M after the home stand, Barnett would gain support from a former president and would be shunned by a governor who was rumored to have national aspirations. The emerging role of politics in the ongoing CU scandal would become painfully clear to him.

Chapter Nine
Presidents, Governors
and Grand Juries

More than a dozen members of the 2004 University of Colorado football team grew up in Texas. For some of them, the road trip to Texas A&M would be a chance to see family and friends. Others looked forward to traveling to a stadium where their team had never lost a game.

Through the first seven weeks of the season the players—at least on the outside—didn't show any effects from the scandalous allegations that would, by the end of the season, expand to include accusations of financial mismanagement in football camps run by coach Gary Barnett and allegations that the money from the camps was part of some secret "slush fund." The players and coaches mentioned what they often-termed "all the bullshit" only when asked about it. They seemed focused on the fact that while the team had a 4-2 record going into the A&M game, its offense had struggled and its defense had given up too many big pass plays. If the cloud of scandal was affecting them emotionally, they weren't showing it. It was hard to imagine, however, that the anger and pain of dealing with both the allegations and fan abuse wasn't boiling up in the players.

Those emotions would have to erupt at some point.

That point would be deep in the heart of Texas.

In geographic terms Boulder, Colorado, and College Station, Texas, are separated by a distance of 823 miles.

Culturally, however, the distance between the city that is home to the University of Colorado and the city that is home to Texas A&M University could better be measured in light years. The two are as different as the Land Rovers that crowd Boulder's

Baseline Road and the giant diesel-powered pickup trucks that roll down College Station's George Bush Drive. Politically the two cities could not more different.

In Boulder a home football game is a big deal to the mostly out-state CU fans at Folsom Field, but of limited interest in many parts of Boulder. The town doesn't exactly turn into Columbus, Ohio, on football Saturdays.

College Station does turn into another Columbus. Football Saturday takes on religious overtones there and has almost as many rituals. On a campus where greeting strangers with the word "Howdy" is almost a rule, nearly everything surrounding Texas Aggie football is done strictly according to tradition.

Thousands of students gather at midnight before every home game for the traditional Midnight Yell.

Those same students render many of Kyle Field's 82,600 seats useless as they stand for the duration of the game, symbolizing a "12th Man" standing at the ready in case he is needed. When a ball is kicked into the end zone and there is no return, the stadium announcer even gives credit for the tackle to the 12th Man.

The 2,100-strong Corps of Cadets marches into the stadium before each game behind the lead of the Corps' highest-ranking officer, a Collie dog whose name is always Reveille.

Hand signals—a thumb pointed upward—exhort the Aggie players to "Gig 'Em."

A "boot line" of knee-high booted senior Corps members wearing spurs greets the team as it returns to the field after halftime.

All-male yell leaders spark a din in what is probably the loudest stadium in college football.

October 23, 2004 was even more stereotypically American than most Saturdays in College Station.

The presidential election was coming down the home stretch.

Two prominent Republican Texans, former President George Bush and current Colorado Governor Bill Owens, were scheduled to attend the Big 12 game between the Texas Aggies and the Colorado Buffaloes.

Bush, an avid Aggie fan, sat in the stands only a few long field goals away from his own presidential library and Owens sat in the luxury box of a friend. In the southeast corner of the stadium sat a couple thousand Colorado Buffalo fans. All were about to see what would end up as one of the best Big 12 games played during the 2004 season, but the political overtones were also hard to miss.

Owens, a graduate of Stephen F. Austin College who also held a master's degree from A&M's biggest rival, the University of Texas, had been as outspoken critic of the beleaguered CU football team. When the scandal allegations exploded early in 2004 he called the football team an "embarrassment" to the state of Colorado. CU football coach Gary Barnett, who was at the center of the controversy, didn't know Bush and Owens would be at the game. It had been all business since the team plane touched down 98 miles away in Houston on an unusually-muggy Friday afternoon.

College Station, with a population of about 70,000, is a tough place to find a hotel room on a football weekend. The teams coming to play the Aggies don't even try. All of them, CU included, stay at the Del Lago Resort, which is on the shores of Lake Conroe and about 40 miles southeast of College Station. The cultural difference between that area and Boulder was clearly drawn on the balcony of every room at Del Lago, where signs read, "No barbecuing on balcony." They could have put a similar warning on the sidewalks, which were nearly as hot as a barbecue grill.

"It usually starts cooling off here by October, but it's staying hot longer this year," CU defensive coordinator Mike Hankwitz said when the team arrived. Hankwitz, who seemed amused at others' amazement over the heat, knew what he was talking about. He had earlier spent six seasons as the coordinator of A&M's famous "Wrecking Crew" defense. "You should feel it in the summer," he said.

No thanks, I told him.

The players seemed loose and almost jovial on the night before a game that could well decide the fate of their season. At the team dinner conversations were louder and more animated than they had been during earlier pre-game nights.

During that dinner a CU staff member appeared in the dining room wearing khaki shorts that, unlike those being worn by most of the coaches and other staff members, were short and almost tight. In an era of baggy shorts, he looked like something out of a 1980 NBA highlight film.

"Nice shorts," Barnett laughed at him. "If the Brothers see that, they will eat you up." Barnett was right. He took the guy over to a table where several black players were eating and they hooted with laughter.

"They're in an awfully good mood tonight," I told Barnett as the players ate. "Are you worried about their concentration?"

"It's hard to gauge that," he said.

As darkness fell, it was also difficult to gauge the difference between the moisture hanging in the street lights and actual rain. A few CU fans made a late-night trip up to College Station to see the famous Midnight Yell.

In the morning the sidewalks at Del Lago were wet. Outside the hotel, CU sports information director Dave Plati was already loading up a van to transport the portable media-relations office to Kyle Field, about an hour away.

"It's raining hard in College Station," he said.

It was also starting to rain again at Del Lago. Maybe the weather wouldn't be hot that day, I thought.

As the four busses carrying the team pulled away, it began to rain hard as a team of six motorcycle police formed an escort. Unlike the escort the Buffs had gotten at Missouri, which consisted of one cop driving his car to the stadium without his flashing lights, this escort was impressive. The motorcycle cops, equipped with rain gear, seemed oblivious to the weather, racing ahead and weaving in and out of traffic to clear the way for our motorcade.

At times they raced through what seemed like several inches of rain on the road. Sitting next to offensive coordinator Shawn Watson in the front row of the bus, I watched the motorcycles weave in and out of the rain and traffic at what seemed to be an unsafe speed. Watson just stared ahead, but I couldn't help being impressed by the riding skills of the Texas Highway Patrol. Had motorcades in Texas been that efficient 40 years ago, President Kennedy might well have died of old age, I thought. As the motorcade reached College Station the rain stopped, but it was easy to see that it had been raining hard. The sides of concrete buildings were soaked. The temperature had fallen to 72 degrees, but that would be the low for the day. The sun was coming out.

For one CU player, however, something much bigger than football was looming like a dark cloud. Defensive end James Garee was carrying more than his travel bag with him on that bus. As the bus turned the corner a block form Kyle Field, thousands of burgundy-clad Aggie fans clogged the streets, but two black jerseys carrying the number 82 stuck out of the crowd. They were worn by Jack and Shirley Garee, the parents of James Garee. Few outside the team knew that Jack Garee was battling terminal cancer and didn't have long to live. The Garees, however, had been at every game so far. As we turned the corner I wondered if James had seen his folks there and wondered what he must have been thinking. The father was battling for his life while the son was about to battle for his team's Big 12 survival while dealing with the impending death of his dad. It must be tough for him, I thought.

A few hours later I would get to see just how tough.

As the team dressed and taped in the visitors' locker room, Kyle Field began to fill up. The attendance would later be announced as just under 74,000. The place wasn't sold out, but still held about 20,000 more people than did Folsom Field when full. There was no TV coverage. Prior to the game, Barnett was interrupted by an unexpected visitor, a Secret Service agent. Former President George Bush was in the stands and wanted to meet him. Barnett accompanied the agent across the field and was introduced to the former president.

"We talked for a few seconds and he gave me a couple words of support," Barnett would later say while refusing to divulge exactly what Bush had told him. Others said Bush's words of support contained some salty language about the way Barnett had been treated in the past year.

Unlike Bush, who was seated in the stands, Colorado Governor Bill Owens had a seat in a friend's suite. And, unlike Bush, he made no effort to see Barnett before the game. Given his criticism of the team and the university, Owens was an unlikely fan that day. He had played a role, and over the next few months would play an even greater role, in the political intrigue behind the so-called CU recruiting scandal.

The folks at A&M were apparently well aware of both the scandal and the political backdrop of CU's problems. The Aggies had scheduled a halftime tribute to their female "recruiting ambassadors," but had contacted Barnett earlier in the week and offered to postpone that tribute until another day. They didn't want to embarrass Barnett or CU. Barnett, while impressed with the gesture, declined. "Go ahead and do what you were going to do," he told them. "We won't be embarrassed because we didn't do anything wrong." Unlike Colorado's governor, Barnett was not embarrassed by his team.

As governor, Owens had done more than just call the team an embarrassment to the state. It was Owens who, in the summer of 2004, appointed Colorado Attorney General Ken Salazar as a special prosecutor to investigate claims of sex assault, providing prostitutes to recruits and other wrongdoing in the CU football program. That grand jury handed up a single indictment charging former part-time CU recruiting aid Nathan Maxcey with hiring prostitutes for himself and for misusing a university cell phone in doing so. The same grand jury refused to charge him with hiring prostitutes for recruits, an allegation brought by self-proclaimed Boulder County hooker Pasha Cowan. When the grand jury finished its work and disbanded, it appeared the seemingly endless string of investigations was over. An independent investigative commission had also failed to connect the CU coaches to any illegal activity, but criticized both the CU administration and the regents for lax oversight.

The grand jury had also written a scathing report that accused CU of lukewarm compliance with its request for records and criticized Barnett for allegedly not turning over all the financial records for his football camps. Denver District Judge Jeffrey Bayless sealed the report, but the Colorado Attorney General's Office seemed hell-bent on releasing it and appealed the decision to seal the document. The appeal would soon prove to be moot. On February 28, 2005, a copy of the report made its way to Denver's Channel 9 and the next morning portions of it appeared in the *Denver Post*, Channel 9's "partner."

Almost immediately the airwaves and the pages of the Denver-Boulder area newspapers were filled with stories based on the report and which claimed Barnett had not complied with subpoenas issued by the grand jury. The report's mention of the use of a series of cash boxes used to make change at Barnett's football camps led to the media referring to the money in those boxes as a slush fund. The stories also alleged that, according to the grand jury report, two female former athletic trainers had been either sexually assaulted by or had engaged in inappropriate sexual relationships with a former coach. Because of the seal, both CU and Barnett were precluded from defending themselves, but not for long. Bayless, angered by the leak, ordered an investigation into its origin and granted CU permission to answer questions raised by the leaked report.

The *Rocky Mountain News* actually interviewed Barnett to get his explanation. But the paper sent sports reporter B.G. Brooks, not a news reporter, to do the story. While the contents of the grand jury report had been trumpeted on the paper's front page, Barnett's response was placed on page 6. In that article Barnett admitted that his faith in the legal system had been shaken by the leaking of the report. He said his faith had proven to be blind. Barnett also disagreed with the notion that he had failed to turn over the financial records of his football camp to the grand jury, saying the panel didn't even ask for the 1099 forms, or earnings reports, of those who worked at the camp. He said he had forms for everyone who was ever paid by the camps, but that the grand jury report made it sound as though they had been requested and denied.

Barnett also defended the use of cash boxes used to make change at the football camps, saying some campers paid their fees in cash and that the boxes were needed to make change and that every penny had been accounted for. Months later, in April 2005, Barnett's sense of humor would take over when he would use the situation to break up the crowd at a meeting of the Buffalo Belles, a women's booster club in Boulder. While accepting a check from the group on behalf of the university, he pulled out a cash box and opened it. The crowd lost it.

The cash-box controversy was hard to understand. Barnett's process sounded awfully similar to the process used by band parents selling concessions at high school basketball games or boosters raising money for a Little League team. Suddenly it was something bad. The media had somehow changed a cash box used to make change at a football camp into a slush fund. It also seemed strange that Barnett was being questioned about the finances of his camps, which are, under the terms of his contract, a private business operated solely by him. That arrangement has never been a secret and is spelled out in his contract, which is a public document that any reporter could have obtained. As part of its contract with Barnett, the university pays him about $200,000 a year to operate the camps, which are owned by him. Barnett writes checks to the camp account as needed, using money the university paid him for that very purpose. It's that simple, but apparently not to the media. An investigation that began as a probe of the activities at the December 7, 2001 party at Lisa Simpson's apartment had expanded to include the scrutiny of Barnett's football-camp finances. Why were the camps being audited and investigated? Why was Barnett being criticized for putting the money he was paid to run the football camps into those camps? Were reporters persisting because they were on a witch hunt and weren't going to stop until they found a witch? They had stepped on themselves before in their quest for that witch.

Several months before the grand jury report was leaked, an audit report was leaked that indicated Barnett paid out most of the profit from the camps to salaries for coaches and bonuses for their wives. That same audit revealed that Barnett had written a $9,000 check to the daughter of assistant coach Brian Cabral for her tuition at the University of Kansas. While he had never made it public, Barnett had been paying college expenses for the children of his assistant coaches since he had been at Northwestern. The guy was getting beaten up for giving away his own money. He could keep every penny if he wanted, but that fact went unreported.

In the interview with Brooks, Barnett once again pointed out that the $200,000 he puts into the camps annually comes from his salary and not a penny comes from CU funds. Barnett said he charges the campers and pays expenses but still has to put in his own money—from funds he is paid for that purpose. He said he deposited about $800,000, or $200,000 a year, into the camp account during his first four years at CU.

Barnett also told the *Rocky* he had all the tax returns from his camps and had offered to allow authorities to inspect them. He claimed everything was above-board and appropriate, while admitting that his accounting practices were primitive.

When Bayless lifted the gag he had placed on CU and Barnett when the secret grand jury report was still a secret, CU President Elizabeth Hoffman also came out swinging in defense of the camp money as one of her last acts as president. A week later she would resign her job under the pressures of both the football investigations and the controversy of allegedly terror-friendly professor Ward Churchill. Hoffman openly challenged the attorney general's office to "set the record straight immediately" regarding the report's allegations that the university did not comply with the grand jury subpoenas.

"We emphatically reject any assertions that the university failed to cooperate with its investigation," she said in a statement. "Assertions that we willfully failed to provide documents are simply untrue and they unjustifiably damage the university's reputation."

Ironically and conveniently, the attorney general's office used grand jury secrecy to avoid answering questions about Hoffman's allegations. In a March 2 *Rocky Mountain News* article, Deputy Attorney General Jason Dunn said his office couldn't comment on the sealed report, even though it had been leaked to the public. How convenient. The attorney general's office, which is still fighting for the release of the report, is on a very short list of entities that could have had access to or leaked it. Extensive excerpts published in the *Denver Post* sounded little like something written by regular folks serving on a grand jury and sounded like something written by lawyers. When I read those excerpts it appeared to me that they were designed to be leaked.

That same *Rocky* article also quoted prominent Denver attorney Scott Robinson, but his words appear to have fallen on deaf media ears. Robinson pointed out that grand juries are historically one-sided in that only the prosecution offers evidence. He also reminded readers that the report was issued by grand jurors who did not have enough evidence for additional indictments. Robinson urged the public to look at the leaked report cynically because it was written strictly from a prosecutorial standpoint—something the reporters who leaked it certainly didn't do.

Releasing sealed grand jury material is a crime in Colorado, but that didn't seem to bother the reporters who had ignored the thousands of pages of public documents that would have cast the "scandal" in a much different light. They were more than willing to go along with a report by a grand jury that failed to indict even one current CU employee or player. Those who appear before grand juries are stripped of most of the rights they enjoy outside a grand jury room, a situation allegedly balanced by the secret nature of the proceedings. The theory is that it's all right to compel testimony in a grand jury proceeding because the results of that testimony will not come back to bite those who give the testimony or those accused of, but not charged, with crimes. That system went sideways in this case and the media helped. And CU stood nearly defenseless against more unsubstantiated allegations.

Other public officials also made hay from the leaked grand jury report. Joyce Lawrence, a former Republican state legislator from southern Colorado who was a co-chair of the Independent

Investigative Commission and who has presumably not read the report, told the *Pueblo Chieftain* she and the commission had been stabbed in the back by Barnett and the university. In a March 9, 2004 story by *Chieftain* reporter Peter Roper, Lawrence said Barnett should be fired because he stabbed the commission in the back by not telling it about the cash boxes.

Lawrence failed to mention that Barnett spent nearly six hours being questioned by the IIC and answered every question thrown at him. She also revealed to the world her ignorance of Barnett's contract, the nature of the football camps and Barnett's private ownership of them. Her reference to "all the money going into the program" also exposed her lack of knowledge. The camp money doesn't go and never has gone into the football program.

Lawrence should have educated herself about the financial makeup of the football camp, which is nearly identical to that on virtually every other big-school football campus in the nation. She didn't know Barnett is paid about $200,000 per year to support his camps. She didn't know the camps also get revenue from the campers in the form of registration fees and things like candy-bar sales. And she apparently didn't know that the camper fees are usually insufficient to cover the camp expenses and that Barnett periodically—and legally—deposits most or all of the $200,000 in contract money to pay those expenses. It is his money. He is literally taking it from one of his pockets and placing it in the other. As mentioned above, he has deposited nearly $800,000 of the camp money into the camp account. That didn't keep Fox-TV personality Bill O'Reilly from referring to it as an $800,000 slush fund. A slush fund, by legal definition in Colorado, is illegal, but virtually every media entity has used the phrase to describe Barnett's camp money.

Roper, who wrote the Lawrence article, fell in lockstep with the brand of journalism being passed off as acceptable. He committed the cardinal journalistic sin of writing a "one-source story" that contained serious allegations but failed to quote even one other person. He didn't call Barnett or CU, but his story was front-page material in Pueblo, where readers of the *Chieftain* were robbed of anything resembling balanced or fair reporting.

Lawrence wasn't the only public official who reacted to the leaked grand jury report. After its release Governor Bill Owens quickly called a meeting with John Suthers, who had been named Colorado Attorney General after Salazar was elected to the U.S. Senate. Owens said he wanted to see if there was a need for another investigation. So far only one Colorado journalist, a sports columnist, has questioned the governor, his motives or his track record regarding CU. Neil Woelk, a sports columnist for the *Boulder Daily Camera*, has never been a Gary Barnett fan. He has criticized the coach repeatedly over the years, but on March 5, 2005 he let the governor have it. Scornfully advocating that common sense rear its head, he called for Owens to cease his attacks on CU and cited the laundry list of investigations and audits that had failed to substantiate allegations of wrongdoing.

Woelk then hit Owens where no one else had dared to go. He called Owens "Governor Billy Bob" and called for Owens' personal conduct to be scrutinized.

Woelk's references to Owens' family values hypocrisy were as close as any reporter has come to scrutinizing the governor's own moral conduct, a subject reporters have inexplicably ignored in the face of whisperings and rumors that have dogged Owens since he separated from his wife of 28 years in 2003. Owens, who cancelled two speeches before social conservative groups shortly after the separation, has refused to comment on his conduct prior to the separation. In a March 6, 2005 interview with the *Denver Post*, he refused to talk about the separation and called the whispers blatantly untrue. The *Post*, of course, couldn't bring itself to mention what those rumors were. Perhaps the paper was correct in not mentioning the rumors about Owens. If so, why did it not show similar restraint when spreading unsubstantiated allegations of rape against unnamed CU players? Its discretion was certainly selective. The governor was treated much differently than were the football players at CU. Weeks later, the alternative weekly *Westword* would publish an almost tongue-in-cheek list of 15 of the biggest rumors about the governor, but they were presented in a humorous manner that intimated that many of the rumors were obviously off the mark. It wasn't a serious investigation of the governor's conduct.

While the mainstream media was giving Colorado's supposedly squeaky-clean governor a pass, those on Internet chat boards were not so kind. Many of those online critics identify themselves as Republicans and GOP donors. One poster identifying himself as a 1987 graduate of CU's law school posted a letter he also sent to Owens in which he claimed that unsubstantiated allegations such as those bandied about by Owens had hurt many fine young men, as evidenced by what he called termed the abusive treatment of the team by the fans in the stands.

"CU players were subjected to the most vile, disgusting and offensive treatment imaginable from fans in opposing stadiums last year," the CU law grad wrote. "I have heard that you attended the CU/Texas A&M game last year. Maybe you didn't hear the taunts of the team that so embarrasses you from the luxury boxes, but the players did."

Actually, the players were lucky at A&M. It is nearly impossible to hear individual voices in the din of Kyle Field.

The writer also notes the lack of arrests or publicity when "200 students stand outside Farrand Hall at CU last year and openly smoke marijuana while the Boulder and campus police looked on and did nothing. Personally, I don't care if college kids smoke dope. You may as well ask them to stop eating pizza. But ask yourself this: If it was 100 football players doing the same thing, would the reaction be similar? Of course not."

In the same letter, the CU booster threatens that "in the event another investigation is ordered by your office, I will pull my support from the Colorado Republican Party and you in particular."

Another long-time, high-ranking CU official who calls himself a Republican and a conservative, told me he recently returned a fund-raising letter sent to him by the Republican National Committee with a note that said, "Not another penny until Bill Owens is no longer the governor of Colorado. He is ruining our state."

Oddly, CU had found itself the target of a political alliance that included a governor who has often said there are too many liberals at CU and liberals who think the football program should be dismantled. The late Everett Dirksen, a Republican Senator from Illinois, was fond of using the expression which says "politics creates strange bedfellows." In this case it certainly appears to have done exactly that in a state with a conservative governor and a liberal flagship university.

Political squabbles, lawsuits and scandal, however, were about to be set aside for game that would last over four hours and which would bring about a flood of heartbreak and emotion for the Buffs

While Aggie fans brought ritualistic tradition to every home game, in 2004 they also had a very good football team with a talent level obscured by the attention being given to Big 12 South powerhouses Texas and Oklahoma. A&M, with a Number 17 national ranking, was 5-1 and had a 3-0 conference record. CU, which was 4-2 and only 1-2 in conference games, had a chance to separate itself from what was considered a sub-par Big 12 North field. A&M also had a very good quarterback who, like his team, had not received the attention afforded the league's other top quarterbacks. Junior Reggie McNeal was big, fast, smart and had a good arm.

Both teams were in for an afternoon they would not soon forget.

Lining up in the "shotgun" formation in which he stood about five yards behind the line of scrimmage, McNeal took the game in hand on A&M's opening drive. Throwing short passes and running when the opportunity arose, he drove his team to the CU 32-yard line before missing on a fourth-down pass. CU did nothing on its first drive and held the Aggies to three plays on their second possession. The defenses were dominating what was shaping up as the most physical game of the season. On its second possession CU started to move the ball, thanks in large measure to a 41-yard run by running back Bobby Purify. It was Purify's longest run of the season and the longest run the Aggies had given up. But the CU drive stalled inside the A&M 10-yard line and the Buffs settled for a 29-yard Mason Crosby field goal to take a 3-0 lead with 7:28 left in the first quarter. Neither team could move the ball the rest of the first quarter, but Purify came to the rescue in the second quarter when he caught a short pass from Joel Klatt and raced down the sideline for a 35-yard gain. But the drive stalled again near the Aggie goal line and Crosby kicked a 26-yard field goal to put CU up by a score of 6-0.

A&M took a 7-6 lead late in the second quarter on a 3-yard Courtney Lewis run set up by a 51-yard wide-receiver pass from Jacob Young to Byron Jones, but CU had one more chance before halftime. Klatt completed five passes and wide receiver Bernard Jackson completed another on a drive capped by a 15-yard touchdown pass from Klatt to Evan Judge. CU ended the first half with a 13-7 lead, but the heat, the humidity and the Aggies were not about to go away. The second half would be a long one for both teams.

The CU locker room looked like a hospital at halftime. I counted eight players with needles sticking in their arms as they took intravenous fluids before dragging themselves back onto the field. Team chaplain Mike Spivey, who usually grabbed a bottle of Gatorade for himself and another for me at halftime, grabbed four bottles. We both drank two. The heat and humidity got even worse as the afternoon dragged on.

After taking the second-half kickoff, Colorado used a 36-yard pass from Klatt to Blake Mackey to move to A&M's 24-yard line and Klatt hit Evan Judge for a 24-yard touchdown pass on the next play. A two-point conversion pass failed, but the underdog Buffs suddenly had a 19-7 lead. Seven plays later the Aggies answered with a field goal that made the score 19-10. The rest of the third quarter was a physical battle in which neither team could prevail, but A&M managed a field goal on the first play of the fourth quarter to make the score 19-13. The Aggies took a 20-19 lead with just over 11 minutes left in the game when Courtney Lewis scored on a 2-yard run. A&M added a field goal with just over four minutes left in the game to take a 23-19 lead.

As CU took the field for its last possession of the fourth quarter, Governor Owens was otherwise occupied. He had made his way down to the section where CU's fans were sitting and was making his way through the crowd shaking hands. In light of what he had earlier said about the team being an embarrassment to the state, his reception was lukewarm. The parents hadn't forgotten his earlier comments.

"I wanted to go up and ask him what my son did to embarrass the state," the mother of one player later said.

"I wanted to smack him," said another.

CU's Buffs didn't notice Owens. They had only four minutes left in which to reclaim the lead. They would do just that, but perhaps a bit too quickly. Klatt threw passes to Purify, Dusty

Sprague, Joe Klopfenstein and Ron Monteilh before Purify scored on a short run with 1:09 left. The Buffs were up 26-23 and A&M had only a minute in which to tie the game and force overtime. That would be plenty of time for McNeal, who passed and ran his team to the CU 2-yard line before Todd Pegram tied the game at 26 as the clock ran out. The ensuing overtime would be a physical battle of wills between 22 young men sapped by the heat and humidity of a South Texas afternoon.

A&M began the overtime with a field goal that gave the Aggies a 29-26 lead, but the Buffs were in a position to win with a short touchdown. At worst, they thought, they could kick a field goal and force a second overtime. But that was not going to happen. On the third play, Purify fumbled on the A&M 11-yard line. The Aggies' Lee Foliaki recovered and the game was over.

Tempers flared as the game ended and the two teams had to be separated by their coaches and referees. CU's players stood stunned and angry before trudging off the field in the wake of a nearly-four-hour battle they had lost.

Only one word could describe the CU locker room after game.

Devastation.

The blood and sweat shed on the field mixed with the tears of defeat as the players flopped onto the locker room benches. Most stared straight ahead for what seemed like an eternity. Some got angry. Fullback Lawrence Vickers lost it, throwing his helmet against a wall. From the back of the room an angry voice screamed, "I can't believe we lost to them bitch-ass muthafuckas."

Some players sat at their cubicles, looking down and sobbing uncontrollably.

It had finally happened. The emotions of the previous nine months had exploded. At the time, the loss seemed to have torn the team apart at the seams. It seemed like the pain and emotion of the allegations had also come home to roost. It looked to me as though the team had finally cracked under the pressure.

How was Barnett going to keep his players focused after such a devastating loss? What could he possibly say to console his team? He quickly climbed up on a bench and got his team's attention. He chose the perfect words.

"Seventy-two men came down here today and played their hearts out," he said. "We gave it everything we had and it just didn't work out. I'm proud of all of you and you should be proud of yourselves. We're going to walk out of here with our heads up and pick each other up."

That was a tall order.

James Garee, whose ill father stood just outside, was inconsolable. So were a lot of the other players. When the players finally emerged from the locker room, they were embraced by their family and friends. Tears were still flowing freely.

Then I saw something that told me a lot about Texas A&M fans. A middle-aged white man wearing an Aggies T-shirt approached a black woman wearing CU colors.

"Tell yer gaahs they were very gallant out they-ah today" he told her in a thick Texas drawl.

Then he hugged her. I gained a large measure of respect for the A&M fans when I saw that. In spite of what some may have spewed on deaf ears during the game, most seemed to respect the game and the men who play it—including their opponents. The dust-up between the exhausted players at the end of the game faded quickly and the few vile hecklers who dotted the stands couldn't be heard on the loud sideline anyway. It had been a great college football game and the Aggie fans appreciated that.

Later, as I sat alone in the nearly-empty press box high above now-empty Kyle Field, I realized that I was losing the sense of detachment I had sworn to keep intact during my three months with the team. Those kids were starting to seem like my kids. I worried about James Garee and his family. I worried about how the players would react to this devastating loss. I worried about my own objectivity, but realized that I had covered people I couldn't stand many times over the years. I saw nothing wrong with covering a group of people I actually respected.

The CU football team came to Texas with a chance to defeat a Top 20 team on the road and to establish itself as a conference contender. It headed back to Boulder with serious questions about its quickly-deteriorating season and the prospect of a home game with Top-Five powerhouse Texas in seven days.

Being at home, however, would offer no relief for the Buffs.

Chapter Ten
Face Down In a Ditch

T hings weren't going to get any easier for the CU football team following its heart-breaking overtime loss at Texas A&M. The Buffs had only a few days of practice to prepare for a visit from the highly-ranked Texas Longhorns. The locker room was quiet as the players showered and dressed after each practice leading up to the game.

Few players paused to look at the bulletin board that had been hanging on the end of a row of lockers all season. They had all read its contents before.

The bulletin board was full of articles clipped from newspapers and the Internet. Those stories weren't about football, however. Every article was about college football players all over the country who had gotten in trouble with the law. Above the bulletin board are the words "Mother's Board." Head coach Gary Barnett, who instituted the board, also named it.

"I tell the players that is what your mother will read if you get in trouble," he said of the ever-present reminder-board that brought back memories of 2002, when four CU players were charged with contributing to the delinquency of minors by bringing alcohol—and in one case a joint of marijuana—to the now-infamous party at Lisa Simpson's apartment. After the party Simpson told police she had been sexually assaulted by unknown men while she was passed-out drunk. Allegations of a gang rape by a group of CU football players and recruits didn't result in criminal charges, but they did result in a federal lawsuit against the school by Simpson and Anne Gilmore, who also claimed to have been raped at the party. The allegations also brought more unsubstantiated accusations of sex assault by football players and incurred both the scorn of victim advocates and the wrath of a district attorney who claimed she warned CU of such incidents four years before the Simpson party.

The allegations also made local and national headlines that painted the CU football program as an orgy of alcohol and sex overseen by a coach who didn't see or didn't want to see what was going on behind his back. Reporters anxious to beat their competitors in what appeared to be an accusation-of-the day contest failed to go beyond the salacious accusations to find out how Barnett actually ran his program.

Beginning with his days as the coach at Air Academy High School near Colorado Springs, he had carried the label of a disciplinarian. Within the coaching profession he was known as a straight-laced, by-the rules guy. Lee Hitchcock, who coached high school football in Colorado for more than 30 years and who coached against Barnett when both were rookie high-school head coaches, called Barnett "a straight-up, strong-character guy whose actions back up his words."

According to records supplied by the university, Barnett backed up his word 48 times during his first four years as CU's head coach. The two-page document details four dozen disciplinary actions ranging from one-game suspensions to scholarship revocation and, in two cases, permanent dismissal from the team. The 48 actions were taken against 34 different players, with four players suspended more than once for academic reasons. Discipline issues, which included violations of team ruled and minor violations of the law, accounted for 25 of the suspensions. Academic deficiencies accounted for nine of the 48 suspensions and two were the result of a combination of academic and discipline issues. Five players were punished by loss of their scholarships during that period and two were kicked off the team permanently. Four of the five scholarship revocations were a result of the Simpson party.

One of those kicked off the team permanently was backup quarterback Colt Brennan, who in April of 2004 was arrested after, by his own admission, he exposed himself to a woman he was on a date with after she invited him to her room. Brennan said he was drunk at the time. He later pleaded guilty to trespass and burglary charges and was never convicted of a sex crime, but his days at CU were over. Barnett quickly kicked him off the team. Brennan had paid for his stupidity with a criminal record and what seemed the likely end of his Division One football plans before eventually ending up at the University of Hawaii.

In the wake of the Simpson party, CU officials erred on the side of suspension in an atmosphere thick with perceived scandal. Defensive end Marques Harris, who lost his scholarship for a semester because of the party, was suspended a second time in 2004 and never came back to CU. The second suspension came in the spring of 2004 while Barnett was on suspension for his remarks about the kicking ability of kicker Katie Hnida and was not the result of illegal conduct. Harris found himself in the middle of a bizarre situation after a 20-year-Boulder woman allegedly vandalized the car of Vance Washington, a teammate of Harris. Witnesses to the situation said Washington told the woman, a former girlfriend, he would call police if she didn't pay for the damage to his car. The woman reportedly sought out and seduced Harris in the bathroom of a Boulder bar before telling Washington of the tryst, threatening to accuse Harris of rape if Washington persisted in making her pay for the damage. Police investigated the bar incident without filing charges. A CU employee said he was told by police who had viewed a video tape of the surveillance camera in the bar that the contact between Harris and the woman was clearly consensual, but that didn't help Harris. With his coach suspended and the team under scrutiny, he was suspended indefinitely. CU officials refused to reinstate him after Barnett returned from suspension and Harris transferred to tiny Southern Utah, where he could play his senior year without taking a year off. He was later signed by the San Diego Chargers.

While his discretion could be questioned at a time when the team's every move was being scrutinized, Harris was never accused of a crime in connection with the tryst with the woman in the bar. Political correctness, not guilt, precluded his return to the team.

In the aftermath of the Simpson party, CU instituted what are regarded as the strictest recruiting rules in the country. Rules adopted in 2004 prohibit official visits by recruits during the football season, although that rule can be lifted in some circumstances. The new rules prohibit recruits from being escorted by players when there are no coaches around and also institutes a 1 a.m. curfew backed up by a bed-check conducted by assistant coaches. Recruiting was also changed by the implementation of rules that require academically-marginal recruits to be scrutinized for admission by academic officials as well as athletic-department employees.

While Harris and many of the 34 players who made the discipline list never completed their careers at CU, Matt McChesney and Sam Wilder had made it.

McChesney, who attended high school about six miles from the CU campus, was the first football recruit to sign with CU in 2000. Wilder, who grew up in a high-rise apartment building in downtown Dallas, was the last.

The five seasons McChesney and Wilder spent at CU were, to say the least, eventful—on and off the field. Together they went through a 3-8 season, then a Big 12 Championship season that saw them come "this close" to playing for the national championship, followed by a high-profile "scandal" that threatened to bring down the program McChesney had dreamed of playing for since childhood.

As the two fifth-year seniors with NFL dreams prepared to play the University of Texas on the day before Halloween 2004, they still entertained hopes of sharing a third Big 12 North crown. Those hopes, however, were nearly non-existent outside the locker room and appeared slim as the team tried to overcome a heartbreaking 29-26 overtime loss at Texas A&M the week before. Going into the Texas game, the Buffs were 4-3 overall, but had an anemic 1-3 record in the Big 12 North.

While McChesney and Wilder had been thrown together as freshman, the two were drawn closer by the events of the five seasons that would follow. Upon meeting on the first day of fall practice, the two became fast friends.

Too fast, in fact.

"When I first checked into the College Inn for training camp my freshman year, I opened the door to my room and saw this loud, 300-pound guy with a shaved head," Wilder said of his first meeting with McChesney. Wilder, at the time a 240-pound defensive lineman, was scared of his new roommate. That night he called his mother in Dallas.

"You won't believe my roommate," he told her.

Few others believed his roommate, either. McChesney says his high school teachers and coaches didn't believe he would stay eligible long enough to play college football. Even his parents were holding their breath. Matt McChesney had never listened to anyone but Matt McChesney and wasn't about to start taking directions just because he was in college.

"I think I scared Sam," McChesney said of that first meeting. "He told me we probably shouldn't hang out together, but we've been hanging out ever since. He's not my friend. He's my brother."

Hanging out together, however, wasn't always the best of ideas.

Although Wilder is much quieter than the bombastic McChesney, the two had a lot in common. Both played the defensive line, although Wilder would switch to the offensive line in his junior year. And both liked to have fun both within and outside the rules. That propensity nearly cost them their college careers during their sophomore year. The pair got drunk and decided to joy-ride across the CU campus on a bicycle—someone else's bicycle. That bone-headed incident got both of them kicked off the football team and out of school for a semester. Both found out early that their coach, Gary Barnett, was not afraid to discipline players and both must have scoffed when critics complained that Barnett lets his players do anything they want.

It took a lot more than a suspension to rattle the stubborn McChesney. Three years after his suspension, the loudest voice in the CU locker room had yet to be silenced in the face of a season that appeared to be headed for the tank. The Texas game would test both his confidence and that of his teammates.

Indian summer temperatures in the mid-50s greeted CU fans as they began to fill Folsom Field for the game with Texas. So did the pom-poms that had been placed in each of the 50,000 seats but which had curiously been ordered in burnt orange—the Texas colors. Someone in the promotions department had inadvertently ordered the opposing team's colors for the pom-poms. The Buffs had also made some changes for the Halloween-Eve game. At a Wednesday meeting the players voted to take their names off the backs of their jerseys for the first time in over 20 years.

The team was using the motivational tools of the desperate as it appeared to be sinking under the weight of both a teetering season and the ongoing investigations.

During the pre-game meeting at the team hotel, Barnett urged his players to forget about the name on the back of the jersey and to concentrate on the one in the front: "Colorado." As the meeting ended Barnett threw a roll of tape to tight-ends coach John Wristen.

"Wristo," he said, "put a strip of tape across the floor in front of the door." He then told his team, "There are two doors in this room. If you cross this line and leave through this door, you are committed to this team and the name on the front of your jersey." Two hours later he repeated the ritual when he instructed strength coach Greg Finnegan to place a similar strip of tape across the floor by the door and gave his team the same exhortation.

The kickoff was delayed by 10 minutes on the order of ABC-TV, which was waiting for the end of the nationally-televised Oklahoma-Oklahoma State game, but the CU defense looked as though it would dominate the Texas game early. Cornerback Terrance Wheatley gave CU a 7-0 lead when he picked off an ill-advised pass by UT quarterback Vince Young and returned it 37 yards for a touchdown to give his team a 7-0 lead with just over five minutes gone in the game. On its next series Texas moved 51 years in 14 plays before Young threw a desperation pass that was picked off by CU's Lorenzo Sims at the CU 15-yard line. The Buffs ended the first quarter with a 7-0 lead, but wouldn't score again in what would be one of their worst losses of the season. Young was another one of the Big 12's large, athletic quarterbacks and kept the CU defense off balance with both his running and passing. The Texas defense, meanwhile, kept CU's offense off the field.

As the Buffs headed to the locker room at halftime, tempers flared in the hallway outside the team auditorium. Normally-reserved running back Bobby Purify, who had been held to an embarrassing minus-10 yards in a first half that saw his team manage only one first down, blew his stack.

"I'm gettin' tackled in the fuckin' backfield," he yelled out.

There was more yelling in the auditorium.

"We have to execute," quarterback Joel Klatt said as the offensive lineman took their chairs on the auditorium stage.

"We have to execute better," offensive line coach Dave Borbely told his players.

"Start fuckin' executing," Finnegan yelled.

The yelling didn't help. In the second half the Texas defense, coached by former Denver Broncos coach Greg Robinson, continued to dominate. Klatt was sacked and harassed by linebackers who seemed to blitz on every play. As the second half began, a ABC sideline reporter asked Barnett what his team had to do to get back in the game, which they trailed 14-7. "We have to get something going on offense," he said.

They never did.

Texas won the game 31-7 and the Buffs' record dropped to 4-4 and 1-4 in the Big 12.

Barnett knew his team had played its worst game of the season and tried to place the blame on himself. "It's obvious I didn't have my team prepared to play today and we just didn't get anything going on offense and we shot ourselves in the foot," he said. "We weren't ready to play on offense and that's on me." Barnett said his team would have to "scratch and claw to find some positives" and called on his players to "dig a little deeper." It was beginning to look like they had nowhere to dig.

With three games left and this team's bowl chances dwindling, Barnett held himself, not his players, responsible.

That usually wasn't the case when his players had off-the-field problems. Wilder and McChesney, who had been kicked off the team for a semester as sophomores for that drunken bicycle joy-ride incident, could attest to that. So could the four who lost their scholarships after the infamous party at Lisa Simpson's house. Few incidents in recent college football history have received more attention or had more ramifications than that party.

Nationally, however, there have been plenty of incidents involving college football players and the law in recent years. In early 2005 an Arizona State University player was charged with first-degree murder in the shooting death of a former player. Schools such as Nebraska, South Carolina and the University of California also had players arrested in 2004 or 2005. A former player at Washington University in St. Louis, Bobby Collins, Jr., was in 2002 handed a staggering 540-year sentence for the gunpoint rape of a woman.

While no CU players have been charged with sexual assault, even minor misdeeds have been punished by Barnett. In 2004 he suspended a player for the 2004 opener for taking a recruit to a strip club, although no drinking or illegal activity was involved. At the same time he suspended three others for the opener for team-rule violations that have never been made public.

As their careers at CU approached their end, experience had taught McChesney and Wilder that Barnett was serious about his rules. Now five years older, they were glad they had been held responsible. In fact, McChesney now credits Barnett's discipline for saving his football career and perhaps his future.

While achieving all-state status at nearby Niwot High School, McChesney thought he was The Man. At CU, however, he would learn he had a long way to go before becoming *a* man. Never a slave to academics, he was the object of questions by those high school teachers who doubted he would stay eligible. They were almost right.

"I didn't listen to my parents, I didn't listen to my teachers and coaches. I was never good in school," he said of the period from high school to early college. "Everyone said I couldn't do this, but when I'm told I can't do something, it makes me work harder." It didn't at first. "I had a .8 average my first semester," he said. It would take years to rehabilitate that horrendous G.P.A. He admits, "It takes a lot longer to climb out of a hole than it does to climb into one."

Things would get worse for McChesney. In his third year a piece of ductwork fell out of the ceiling during a team meeting and struck him, injuring his shoulder. On the practice field he "blew up" an ankle and had to have surgery. Then there was the incident that got him kicked off the team and out of school for a semester. During that time he took some classes at a local junior college, moved back in with his parents and took a job at the same hardware store where Patsy Ramsey bought the famous paint brushes that made some people think she had killed her 6-year-old daughter JonBenet.

"I worked at McGuckin's (Hardware) for a semester. I came over and watched spring practice. It was the first time I had never had football." McChesney said the experience "ate me up inside" and was humiliating.

"Two other guys had been kicked off the team, but they went back home and nobody saw them. I live here. I had to stay here and let everybody see the situation I was in. It was a real dark time in my life."

McChesney was reinstated the following year and graduated with a degree in history in May of 2005.

Wilder, who graduated with a degree in economics in December of 2004 and who signed as a free agent with the Dallas Cowboys in April of 2005, also credited Barnett and his staff for his maturation.

"I've grown up here in the time since I was 18, because of the coaching staff," he said. "When I got in trouble, they welcomed me back."

McChesney said Barnett taught him, "You've got to be man and do what you said you would do. He had my back and gave me chance to come back and do the things I said I would do here. A lot of places would have let me get away with that stuff."

Barnett apparently taught him something about himself, too.

"The coaches were critical in teaching me things I needed to do, but I also learned that you don't do anything without yourself. I had to make the decision to do the right things."

After the 2004 season ended, both Wilder and McChesney continued their training at CU in hopes of landing a job in the NFL. Together with fellow seniors Ron Monteilh and Bobby Purify, they began commuting daily to Denver to train at Velocity Sports. They were accompanied on those trips by two players who didn't play at CU, Joel Dreesen of Colorado State and Bo Scaife, who grew up in Denver but who attended the University of Texas. McChesney had grown up enough to respect Dreesen, in spite of the open hatred between the two Colorado football teams.

"He's a good guy and a great opponent," McChesney said. "I hope his college team loses every game it ever plays, but I respect him." Dreesen was later selected in the NFL draft, but his CU workout buddies weren't so lucky. While none of CU's seniors were drafted, four of them--McChesney, Wilder, Purify and defensive tackle Brandon Dabdoub—signed free agents contracts with NFL teams the day after the draft.

McChesney, who signed a contact with the St. Louis Rams, had survived a series of injuries and his own stubborn refusal to listen to others earlier in his college career. When asked where he would be had he not played football at Colorado, McChesney's answer came fast.

"Probably face down in a ditch somewhere," he said. "CU gave me the chance to do the things I have done."

While he had matured during his time playing for Barnett, McChesney certainly didn't lose any of his trademark confidence. Four days after the embarrassing loss to Texas, he strutted his way back to the locker room after a practice.

"We have to run the table," he said of the team's three remaining games. "I'm going to get me some more hardware before I leave here," he said in reference to the two Big 12 North trophies his team had won in the past four years.

At the time those seemed the words of a fool. CU's offense seemed to be getting worse, not better. The Buffs faced a road game at Kansas and a home game against Kansas State before finishing their season at Nebraska on the day after Thanksgiving. They would be underdogs in all three games and their chances of winning the Big 12 North looked to be close to zero.

McChesney is crazy, I thought.

He would also prove to be prophetic.

Chapter Eleven
Circle the Wagon

A s October turned into November, the University of Colorado football team was looking at more bad news than good.

The good news for Gary Barnett and his players was that 2004 only had two months left and they could still go to a bowl game and contend for the Big 12 title if they won their last three games. The bad news for them was that 2005 would bring more allegations and more calls for the coach's firing.

As the leaves fell from the trees, it remained to be seen if the team's remaining three games would bring good news or bad. The Buffs had lost four of their five October games and their offense at times looked as though it may not score until 2005.

Even the team's fans were getting restless. Posters on the Internet chat board were calling for changes at quarterback and were also calling for the head of offensive coordinator Shawn Watson. Some were calling for Barnett's job. Colorado Governor Bill Owens, who early in the year called the team an embarrassment to the state, had traveled to the Texas A&M game but hadn't bothered to congratulate the team or its coach after the Buffs played their best game of the year in an overtime loss. Owens, who spent the fourth quarter shaking hands in the stands, made no attempt to contact the team or Barnett after the game.

"I never heard from him," Barnett would later say. Barnett in March of 2005 would meet Owens for the first time. At Barnett's request, the two conversed for more than an hour in Owens' office, but their conversation remained a mystery. Barnett would only say the two talked about baseball and examined the governor's extensive baseball-card collection. Owens gave no details of the meeting, although he and Barnett both characterized it as cordial.

Even the Boulder police were showing no love for the Buffs. In the week leading up to the Texas A&M game, the CU coaches pumped crowd noise into the practice field to simulate the noise at Kyle Field. The cops came and told them to turn it down.

As the players left the field at halftime of their 31-7 home loss to Texas at the end of October, the home crowd booed them. Barnett shook his head in disgust when he talked about the halftime booing nearly a week later. "I couldn't believe it," he said. "I know they were booing me, but I'm not sure our kids knew that."

CU President Elizabeth Hoffman was among the passengers on the team's flight to Lawrence, Kansas, for the game against the University of Kansas. After dealing with the football allegations since late 2001, Hoffman faced another nightmare in 2005 when an essay written by minority studies professor Ward Churchill created a national stir. In that essay Churchill hinted that some of the victims of the Sept. 11 terrorist attacks on the World Trade Center were not innocent and played a role in America's perceived international sins because of their role as what he called "technocrats." While much of the country gasped at what they saw as his pro-terrorism stance, a Boulder speech by Churchill weeks after the essay became a national story was packed with cheering supporters. There are very few places in the country where he could have received such a warm reception. Certainly New York City, which lost thousands of people in the attacks, wouldn't be one of them.

Churchill's essay resulted in calls for his firing by Colorado Governor Bill Owens and more than a few state legislators, but Hoffman defended his right to free speech, no matter how inflammatory it may be. Both Hoffman and members of the university's board of regents said they felt the university would open itself up to a large, successful lawsuit if Churchill were to be fired for his comments. A subsequent investigation into alleged plagiarism and other alleged academic wrongdoing by Churchill was still underway in the spring of 2005, but Hoffman's fate seemed already sealed before the Churchill affair. Beginning with the press conference at which she announced coach Gary Barnett's suspension in February 2004, Hoffman had come under criticism for her handling of the situation. Fans and athletic department employees criticized her for not defending the football program and the university while critics of the football program accused her of turning a blind eye to its sins. Hoffman was in a no-win situation politically and said she hoped her resignation would give CU a fresh start in battling its public-relations problems.

Hoffman's relationship with Barnett apparently didn't warm up after she reinstated him. During that plane ride to Kansas, according to another passenger on that plane, she didn't speak to Barnett unless spoken to, in spite of being seated just across the aisle from him. November was warm compared to the chilly treatment the Buffs were getting both at home and on the road.

In a week in which Colorado returned to Mountain Standard Time, the Buffs were traveling to Kansas on what looked an awful lot like Mountain Borrowed Time. The airport in Lawrence, Kansas is only about a two-hour drive from St. Joseph, Missouri—the spot where 19th-century wagon trains traditionally began their westward journeys. When those processions came under attack, they circled the wagons to form a protective shield. But there didn't seem to be any other wagons in the Buffs' march through the 2004 season. Like the black family forced to bring up the rear of the wagon train in "Blazing Saddles," the Buffs had only one choice when they came under attack.

They circled the wagon.

It was a chore that was becoming increasingly lonely.

Perhaps it was the lopsided loss to Texas. Or maybe Barnett felt he had nothing to lose. But, for whatever reason, he decided to ignore his team's fragile mental state as it prepared for the Kansas game. It became obvious he wasn't going to let his players feel sorry for themselves. During the week of practices prior to the KU game, frigid temperatures caused steam to roll off the heads of the players when they removed their helmets. That was nothing, however, compared to the steam they would see coming from Barnett's ears when they got to Kansas. Barnett had postponed his usual Thursday-night speech to the team and re-scheduled it for after dinner on Friday. Barnett, who looked anything but happy during the team's Friday-night dinner, paced the hallway outside the team meeting room at the Marriott Hotel in Overland Park.

Barnett looked stern as the players filed into the meeting. "If anyone has to take a leak, do it now," he said. "I need your undivided attention." As the last players took their seats, he instructed an assistant to close the door.

"This is the most important thing I'm going to tell you during your career at the University of Colorado," he told them. "Listen well."

All eyes were forward as Barnett began. "You didn't come to CU to change it," he said. "You came here to be changed. The guys who wore your numbers before you put their heart and souls into this program and I want the same from you. Who are you going to listen to?" Barnett said he wanted players who want to be coached and who want to get better. "That's what we had in mind when we recruited you guys. That's the type of player we want," he said. "You've got to say, 'Coach, make me better.'"

Barnett then called on Darian Hagan, a coaching intern who had been the quarterback on CU's 1990 national championship team, to address the team. Hagan recalled the names and the efforts of other former Buff players and challenged the team to live up to their legacy. Assistant head coach Brian Cabral, who played at CU in the late 1970s and who later played on the Chicago Bear's 1985 Super Bowl championship team, also had a few words for the 2004 Buffs.

Normally soft-spoken defensive coordinator Mike Hankwitz wasn't in a mood to coddle his players either. He began his speech to the defensive players by reading aloud a Kansas newspaper story in which CU's defense was called the weakest in the Big 12.

"That is getting old," he said as he slammed own the paper. "We haven't played like we're capable of. It's time to stand and be counted."

Barnett closed the Friday-night meeting not with the usual motivational video, but with a video that contained no pictures— only a dark screen and the voice of Al Pacino addressing his players in a scene from "Any Given Sunday" in which he spoke of life and football both being games of inches.

Just before that Friday-night meeting in Lawrence, I sat down with Barnett to ask him about the increasing calls for changes from both fans and the media.

"That's the temptation, to start making big changes," he said, "but change doesn't happen like people think it can. This is not a video game. You can't make wholesale turns. You just have to keep hitting the stone until it breaks."

Barnett was well aware that his players just might break before the stone, saying their actions were the only way to determine if they were listening to the detractors or to their coaches. "If they're doing what you're asking them to do, they're listening to you," he said. "If not, they are listening to someone else."

He knew his young players were tempted to listen to those who had already written them off.

"While they're young on the field, they're also young off the field," he said. "They have no idea how to react to pressure. They get criticized like they are pros and it's tough for them to handle. They have to learn how to handle this level of pressure and this level of competition."

The Buffs would run into plenty of both the next day.

As the team bus sneaked its way through the surprisingly hilly, tree-lined streets of Lawrence, a vendor was setting up the little snack trailer just inside Memorial Stadium. A sign on top of the trailer advertised Funnel Cakes and Chicken Fingers. The 50,000-seat stadium would that day hold only about 38,000 KU fans. Practice for the basketball season, the premier sport at Kansas, had already begun and it seemed like the football fans were just going through the motions.

Some of the students, however, were tuning up the heckling skills that make nearby Allen Fieldhouse such a tough place for visiting basketball teams to play. KU students, like those at other basketball schools, take heckling seriously. They study media guides and newspapers to glean personal information they can use as courtside smack-talking fodder. In fact, in early 2005 Kansas basketball coach Bill Self had to publicly implore the Jayhawk fans to cease using profane chants at home games.

As the CU team ran on the field for pre-game warm-ups an hour before the kickoff, a small group of KU students in blue T-shirts started heckling from the first few rows behind the visiting bench. At Memorial Stadium only the running track separates the visiting team from the front row. When the stadium is not loud, it's impossible not to hear every word being said. Vile comments greeted the cheerleaders, the players and the coaches. The vitriol initiated by a small group of activists and perpetuated by a media devoid of skepticism had spread across the country.

It was hard to figure how the CU players were able to shrug off the abuse all season without punching someone. While the sexual and sometimes racial taunts rained from the stands, the security guards standing between the CU players and the KU fans stood motionless and did nothing. After someone complained to them about racial slurs, two regular cops went over to the stands and told the fans to knock it off.

The KU fans certainly had a lot to heckle about early in the game. In spite of Barnett's speech the night before the game, the Buffs looked lethargic in the first quarter of a game they had to win to keep alive any hope of a bowl game or a Big 12 North championship. The Jayhawks took only eight plays to go on an 80-yard drive that ended when running back John Randle scored from the 2-yard line. KU was quickly up 7-0.

It got worse for CU after that. On its first play of the day, CU gave the ball back to KU. Klatt's pass was intercepted by Rodney Harris and KU had the ball on CU's 28-yard line. Randle scored again on a 2-yard run three plays later and Jayhawks had a 14-0 lead with only four minutes gone in the game. A commercial on the scoreboard noted that O'Reilly's Auto Parts was donating $15 to charity for every first down the Jayhawks earned during the season. According to the sign, the folks at O'Reilly's had so far donated $1,950. The way the Buffs' defense was playing early, O'Reilly's would be out of business before nightfall.

Colorado punted in short order on its second series and the CU defense was quickly back on the field. CU's defenders had so far not responded to Hankwitz's challenge to stand up and be counted. But they were about to. On the second play of KU's third possession defensive tackle Matt McChesney hit Jayhawk quarterback Jason Swanson hard and knocked him out of the game. McChesney would later tell reporters, "He didn't look too happy when I got off him. I wasn't trying to hurt anyone out there but I got a pretty good lick on him."

The Jayhawks brought in quarterback John Nielsen on the next play and he started off by completing a short shovel pass to Randle. After gaining five yards, Randle was hit by linebacker

Jordan Dizon, but managed to slip from his grasp. As he pulled away from Dizon, his ball-toting left arm was extended. So was CU defensive tackle Vaka Manapanu, who wrapped him up and stripped the ball. The ball bounced twice before landing in the arms of safety Dominique Brooks, who was already heading in the other direction. Brooks raced down the sideline for a 41-yard touchdown and CU was back in the game at 14-7.

After forcing Kansas to punt on its next possession, CU's offense finally put together a drive long enough to give its defense a rest. The Buffs used up nearly eight minutes in going 55 yards on 17 plays before Mason Crosby kicked a 19-yard field goal to make the score 14-10. The first half would end with the score unchanged, but CU would need a much better effort in the second half if they expected to win only their second Big 12 game.

Inside the locker room at halftime, Barnett turned back into Al Pacino.

"You have two choices," he growled. "You can go out and win this game or you can accept the consequences. You have 30 minutes. Keep hitting the stone."

Colorado would take its first lead early in the second half, but it wouldn't last. The CU offense finally got going when Klatt threw a 34-yard pass to fullback Lawrence Vickers to key an eight-play drive that would end with a 4-yard touchdown pass to tight end Joe Klopfenstein. In spite of its horrendous start, CU was up by a score of 17-14. Kansas, however, came back with an 80-yard drive that ended with a 19-yard Nielsen scoring pass to Brandon Rideau. CU was on the short end of a 21-17 score late in the third period.

Neither Kansas nor Colorado could move the ball on their next two series, but CU punt returner Stephone Robinson would turn the game around at the end of the third quarter when he fielded a punt, changed directions and used a block by Dizon to get outside the KU defense and run 48 yards for a touchdown.

Colorado would punt again and suffer through Klatt's third interception of the day before putting together a 10-play drive. A 4-yard Lawrence Vickers touchdown run and a failed extra-point attempt put the Buffs up for good at 30-21. A late Kansas drive would be snuffed out when cornerback Tyrone Wheatley intercepted a Nielsen pass at the CU goal line.

The CU band played the fight song as the clock expired, but played it again seconds later when the CU team gathered a the sideline where the band was sitting. McChesney, who turned 23 years old that day, wanted to lead the band.

"It's my birthday," he yelled as he climbed atop the ladder formerly occupied by the band leader and led the band in the fight song. McChesney's birthday had turned out to be a happy one.

After the game, Barnett was also happy, telling reporters the win gave his team a chance to get a bad taste out of its mouth. Ever the optimist, he told his players, "If Kansas State beats Missouri and Nebraska loses again, then we could be in the driver's seat." Both of those happened that same day and CU was in a position to qualify for a bowl game by splitting its last two games and to actually win the Big 12 North by beating both K-State and Nebraska and getting some help from Missouri.

The point where CU trailed Kansas by 14 points was the closest the team had come to seeing its season ruined, but there was now renewed hope among the players.

But the team would have to circle its own wagons again before the season ended. Barnett's job security would still be an issue in 2005 as audits of his football camp continued while he pushed for a contract extension he claimed was necessary to recruit new athletes. Stephone Robinson, the redshirt freshman whose punt return turned the game around, would need the support of his teammates after twice being targeted by racially-hateful e-mails before spring practice began.

The leaking of the report in the CU grand jury investigation would re-awaken those who had earlier called for Barnett's firing. It would also add a few more detractors to the list. Those detractors would once again be fueled by, of all people, newspaper columnists long on opinions and short on facts. The first weekend in March brought three such columns, all in the *Denver Post*. Longtime *Post* columnist Woody Paige, who moved to New York to work for a couple of ESPN shows and who at that time still wrote one column per week, led the charge.

Paige's column asked readers to envision the image of Barnett riding around with 16 cash boxes in his car, in reference to the football-camp cash boxes that mysteriously became "slush-fund" boxes in every newspaper, TV and radio story since the leaking of the grand jury report. Paige inexplicably stated that there had been a constant cover-up in the CU athletic department and that the cover-up went beyond just the football team but offered no evidence to support those arguments. Who covered up and for what? How did the cover-up go beyond the football team? He didn't answer any of those questions.

In spite of what the leaked grand jury report alleged, the facts show that Barnett's football camp was audited once by a private firm and that he voluntarily turned over the books to Colorado's state auditor. So far no one has found any crimes or misdemeanors connected with the boxes used to make change for camp fees and candy bars. Paige, of course, never mentioned that.

Paige also lambasted the alleged use of alcohol to attract recruits another charge that was even dismissed by the Independent Investigative Committee that spent three months digging for dirt it never found.

Fellow *Post* columnist Mark Kiszla also jumped on board that weekend, announcing in his column that his daughter would never attend CU. He made perhaps the most preposterous statement yet when he said it is difficult to deny that women were being served up like the steaks served at the training table. Where did he get that? The last three years have produced no evidence of that, but irresponsible columnists such as Kiszla continue to make statements that simply aren't true. Where are their editors? How do they get away with writing such drivel? Kiszla, who in April of 2005 was named the national sport columnist of the year, could avail himself of the same documents and records that the Denver-Boulder and the national media have similarly ignored, but he hasn't. Both history and records, including the voluminous documents generated during the various CU investigations, clearly show that no women were served to anyone, whatever that means. Kiszla's assertion was totally irresponsible, but went unchallenged.

It was also hypocritical. While presenting himself as a bastion of virtue, Kiszla failed to mention that he was once stripped of his credentials by the Colorado Rockies and the American Baseball Writers Association after he was caught rummaging through the locker of former Colorado Rockies player Dante Bichette. Reports from eyewitnesses said Kiszla was caught by Bichette's teammates while removing a tube of "andro," a since-banned performance-enhancing substance that was legal at the time, from Bichette's locker. Witnesses said Bichette's teammates came close to beating Kiszla down when they caught him. A couple years later another Rockies player, Mike Hampton, had to be restrained from smacking Kiszla in the parking lot outside Coors Field.

The *Denver Post's* part-time, out-state columnist, Ed Quillen, went a step further than Kiszla or Paige. In his March 13 column he called for CU to drop its football program altogether.

Quillen argued that without football there would no players accused of rape and no scandals involving alcohol, sex or drugs in Boulder.

No players subject to rape allegations? How about no football players subject to false rape allegations? Quillen makes the assumption that the rapes occurred and has already convicted players who were never charged. He argued that if there is no football, there will be no players to accuse. Now, that's air tight logic! Quillen also took a swipe at the graduation of rate of CU's football players, noting that the NCAA placed it at 44 percent. Notwithstanding the fact that the NCAA counts transfers and early NFL entries against the graduation rate.

Even more scandalous was the reaction of some politicians to the rash of "fire-Barnett" columns. During the second week of March 2005, Colorado state legislator Cheri Jahn wrote a letter to the CU regents asking for Barnett's dismissal. The letter, also signed by five other female legislators, said the toleration of sex assault "pierces my heart."

And it should.

The only problem is that there have been no proven—or even or charged—sex assaults against CU players. Apparently the presumption of innocence that lies at the core of the American judicial system was not important in this case.

Ms. Jahn, who claimed in the letter to have a background as a victim advocate, chose to base her argument not on facts, but on Kiszla's column.

She wrote, "As Mark Kiszla wrote his thoughts, I felt a pit in my stomach when I absorbed his words, 'there is a deep-rooted football culture that dehumanizes women on campuses nationwide.'" She took Kiszla's sweeping, unsubstantiated statement and used it to argue for the dismissal of Gary Barnett. Had Ms. Jahn done her homework, she would have discovered that nothing of the sort has ever been proven to exist at CU. Had she spoken with or investigated the background of Barnett, she likely wouldn't have uttered such a statement. But, her letter got lots of attention from the media. Five other legislators hopped on the political-correctness bandwagon and signed off on her ill-informed letter. When her letter became public, Barnett tried to phone Jahn, but she refused to take his call.

Peter Boyles, a Denver radio talk-show host, also bought the accusations hook, line and sinker and became one of the football program's harshest critics. Boyles was not new to bandwagon-jumping. When the JonBenet Ramsey murder investigation was the hot topic in the late 1990s, Boyles had bumper stickers printed that said, "Focus on the Ramsey Family," and openly accused the little girl's parents of killing her. He didn't need any facts to get ratings for his program. He had a catchy bumper sticker. JonBenet Ramsey's parents have since been virtually cleared of suspicion and the media has long since abandoned the story.

When the grand jury that investigated the Ramsey slaying finished its work, Boyles and I were among dozens of reporters who attended a much-anticipated press conference announcing the results of the investigation. I was standing next to him as we waited for then-district attorney Alex Hunter to make the announcement.

"They've indicted John and Patsy Ramsey," Boyles whispered to me as we stood in the crowd. "They are drawing up arrest warrants right now."

"How do you know that?" I asked him.

"A guy from NBC told me," he responded.

Seconds later Hunter took the podium and announced there were no indictments in the case.

"Nice tip, Pete," I told Boyles, who was hoping that the grand jury would come to the same conclusion he had come to in the Ramsey case. His tip was bullshit, but he never went on the air to say he had jumped to a wrong conclusion when he publicly accused the Ramseys of killing their child. Boyles had again shown himself to be ill-informed, but more disturbingly, didn't seem to care.

Kiszla, Paige and Quillen, as well as Jahn and the five other legislators, chose political correctness over factual correctness to further their anti-football argument. While politicians are almost expected to be opportunistic, we should expect more from journalists who hide their bias behind the PC agenda. Columnists are supposed to write their opinions, but often base those opinions on their own petty, personal prejudices. Politicians, of course, are more than willing to drink from the same trough. Meanwhile, the people who think they are getting real news in the papers are, instead, getting used.

Those same journalists are much less willing to crusade when the issues don't fit their agenda. In fact, they became inexplicably invisible when an issue arose at CU that was outside their political and social agenda.

While the media was vilifying scores of young black men falsely accused of rape in the spring of 2004, it virtually ignored the racist threats leveled against those same young men. Virtually the entire CU football team was hit with racist e-mails, but there was no outcry from the media. The threats were barely reported and were ignored by law enforcement officials, including Boulder District Attorney Mary Keenan who has always portrayed herself as a friend of victims.

In the first few months of 2005 the racist threats returned, but once again went virtually ignored by the media. Then, in early March, former CU quarterback and current radio talk show host Charles Johnson revealed, on Boyles' show, that CU punt returner Stephone Robinson had received threatening racist e-mails in February and March. *Rocky Mountain News* sports writer B.G. Brooks, however, was the only reporter in one of the biggest markets on the country to write about the threats. The news reporters who covered the CU situation didn't deem them newsworthy.

In a March 16, 2005 article, Brooks quoted CU football operations director David Hansburg as saying that a year earlier racially-motivated, mass e-mails were sent to the entire team. That was, of course, disturbing. It has also gone unreported for a year. In the article Hansburg told Brooks that Robinson had received two e-mails in a six-week period and that both were racial and threatening.

That revelation came a week after the National Association for the Advancement of Colored People announced it was investigating the racial atmosphere at CU. In February 2004, I had written an article in which the NAACP had made a similar announcement. There was, however, no further action from the NAACP for a year.

While the media effectively ignored the threats against Robinson, the *Boulder Daily Camera* on March 20, 2005 published an article detailing racial tensions at CU. The story contained testimony from a Mexican-American student who claimed she was spat upon and called a "wetback" by a white man as she crossed the campus. The article also quoted Stephanie King, a CU senior who at the time was also a member of the Black Student Alliance, who said the university was sick with racism but that that social ill has gone completely unaddressed.

Those incidents also included an on-campus fight that began with a white student calling a black student a "nigger." Reports said both combatants were charged in the case. Why was the black student charged? Isn't "nigger" considered a fighting word? Disturbingly, the *Boulder Daily Camera* story about racial tension at CU did not mention that the entire football team had been targeted a year ago. It also failed to mention that Stephone Robinson had received two racial-hate e-mails in a recent six-week period. Was his victimization ignored because he was a football player? Was it ignored because he was a man? Was it ignored because he was black? It doesn't really matter. Those are all bad reasons to ignore perhaps the most disturbing incidents of "racial tension."

Where were the rest of the reporters who had been more than willing to print unsubstantiated allegations against the CU football team? Where was the *Denver Post's* Jim Hughes, who was quick to print the one-sided, unsubstantiated contents of the illegally-obtained grand jury report but who didn't seem to care about the rise of racial hatred on the laid-back, liberal CU campus? Where was DA Mary Keenan? Denver's Channel 9, the TV station that "broke" the allegations against CU, said nothing about the racial threats.

The one-sided nature of the CU coverage was never more evident than when the racial threats were divulged.

Where was state representative Cheri Jahn, who made a point of bringing up her background as a victim advocate, and her five cohorts who signed the letter calling for Barnett's job?

Where was the outcry that reverberated across Colorado and the nation in 2004 when it was revealed that CU players had sex with white women? The bias of both the media and Colorado's politicians was clear. Gary Barnett was labeled as an insensitive oaf when he criticized Katie Hnida's kicking abilities, but those who criticized him for politically-incorrect speech were deadly silent when black men were made the victims of hate crimes. It appears that racial hatred is somehow acceptable, while interracial relationships are not. Hypocritical political correctness seems to dictate that you can't call a flight attendant a stewardess, but you can call a black man a nigger.

Colorado Governor Bill Owens has yet to announce that the racial incidents are an embarrassment to the state. He didn't hesitate, however, to use those words when the CU football players were falsely accused of rape.

There is the temptation to write off the actions of the district attorney and others as not being racial. The events of early 2005, however, indicate that race has played an obvious role in the investigation of the football program and in the media's treatment of the CU story.

It seems rather stupid to measure the comparative evils of sexism and racism, but both the actions and inactions of the media and the politicians have given rise to that comparison. Are they racist or are they just sexist? Sexism should not be a defense for racism.

It probably makes no difference to Stephone Robinson and his teammates whether the hatred directed toward them is based on gender or race.

It's still hate.

And it's still no big deal to the media.

Had the media truly been interested in exposing injustice they would have jumped all over the story of CU wide receiver Ron Monteilh, who was the victim of both false identification and vindictive prosecution and whose maddening story was completely ignored by those in the media.

Chapter Twelve
To Kill a Mockingbird

T he Big 12 is a sprawling football conference, stretching east from the Rocky Mountains to the Great Plains and south nearly to the Gulf of Mexico. During the months of September, October and November the weather at Big 12 games can range from stifling heat to bitter cold. During the 2004 season the weather across the Big 12 didn't seem to have a middle ground. There were two types of weather. Too hot and too cold.

CU's Nov. 13 home game against Kansas State was the coldest game the team played all season. Temperatures dipped into the 20s the night before the game and snow fell in the area south of Boulder and Denver.

By the time the Buffs and the Wildcats kicked off to open their 12:30 p.m. game, the temperature had climbed to only 35 degrees. Neither team lacked motivation in their next-to-last Big 12 game of the year. K-State, which had won the Big 12 Championship in 2003 and had embarrassed CU 49-20 along the way, was struggling. The Wildcats had come to Boulder with a 4-5 record and could only qualify for a post-season bowl by winning their last two games.

CU, meanwhile, was in only a slightly better position. The Buffs' come-from-behind win over Kansas the week before had put them only one win away from the six wins required to qualify for a bowl. They were just-barely still in the hunt for the Big 12 North championship. When the team came off the field after the Kansas win, defensive tackle Matt McChesney held up three fingers.

"Three in a row," he screamed. "We're gonna run the table." CU would need wins over both K-State and Nebraska in order to back up McChesney's brash prediction. The K-State game would also be the last home game for a dozen CU seniors. Starters, such as McChesney, Bobby Purify, Sam Wilder and Ron Monteilh, were going to play at Folsom Field for the last time.

Earlier in the week it looked as if McChesney wouldn't play at all. As the team went through weight-lifting drills on Wednesday, McChesney spent most of his time doing wind sprints to the nearest bathroom. He had a bad case of the flu and lost 12 pounds in two days. As the players lifted weights, a video re-play of the team's 49-20 loss to K-State the year before played over and over on the weight-room TV.

The players stopped to watch the part featuring a commercial advertising Bobby T's, a Manhattan, Kansas, restaurant. Bobby T's, according to the commercial, gives away free nachos every time the Wildcats score 49 or more points. In 2003 the Buffs had played a part in treating the K-State fans to free nachos and they weren't happy about it. They were still unhappy about the fact that K-State scored with 38 seconds left while leading 42-20.

Publicly, neither the players nor coach Gary Barnett mentioned 2003's "Nacho Game." But privately, they were seething. In the video shown as a motivational tool on Thursdays, video director Jamie Guy included a shot of the K-State scoreboard announcing the free nachos at the end of the game. He also added a message at the end of the video.

"Enjoy your nachos," it said. "Paybacks are a bitch."

While the Nacho Game had been played in mid 70-degree temperatures in Kansas, CU's paybacks would have to be exacted on a cold, windy field. The Buffs decided to wear their all-black home uniforms, the same ones that had the players' names removed from them before the Texas game. As the players dressed inside the Dal Ward Center, I noticed the names were still missing. I also noticed the players were wearing Nike-issued knee-high white tube socks, a change from the low-cut black socks they had worn in warmer weather. It was nice to see the 1970's-era high socks back in use.

"If the socks are any indication, you guys are going to win today," I told Barnett in the locker room. "It's about time those knee-high tubes made a comeback. They look like real football socks." No one else seemed to care about the socks.

In his pre-game speech, Barnett reminded his team of its season-ending loss to Nebraska the year before and the start of off-season conditioning the day after. He didn't want them to sit home for the bowl season for a second year in a row. "Forty-nine weeks later we are in a position to go to a bowl," he reminded them. "You get to control that. You're right where you want to be." It was also clear that Barnett hadn't forgotten the Nacho Game of 2003. He made a derisive reference to "some restaurant in whatever town that is" and told his team, "I hope they enjoyed their nachos."

While Barnett was telling his team they were right where they wanted to be, Ron Monteilh could have been forgiven for wondering why he was still at CU. The senior wide receiver had gone nine games without a touchdown pass, but the challenges he had faced in Boulder were much bigger than that. Monteilh, a victim of stark misidentification, would soon leave Boulder wondering if he would spend the rest of his life being called a rapist.

Ron Monteilh, Jr., had faced many challenges in his young life. His father died of leukemia in 1991 when Ron, Jr., was only 9 years old. His mother Marissa had raised three children in Inglewood, which was not among the more prestigious ZIP codes in Los Angeles. She worked as a TV news reporter and even acted in commercials in order to earn enough to keep her kids in Catholic school. By the time Ron finished eighth grade at Notre Dame Elementary School, tuition was skyrocketing at the Catholic high schools in LA. She wanted her son to attend St.

Bernard's High School, but, in her words, "It was getting extremely expensive."

Marissa Monteilh, who described herself as "someone who always wanted something beyond a 9-to-5 job," had to get creative in looking for a school for her kids. She noticed newspaper ads featuring rents in parts of Beverly Hills that were about the same as in L.A. "We found an apartment in Beverly Hills that was almost in Los Angeles and the rent wasn't any higher," she said. A new address in the 90210 ZIP code wouldn't make the family any more prosperous, but it would make Marissa feel much better about her son's school. Besides, the coaches at Beverly Hills High were accustomed to "L.A. kids" coming to their school and, according to Marissa, "took the time to make sure the minority kids were adjusting."

It didn't take Ron long to adjust. He became an instant sensation on the football field, prompting a Los Angeles sportswriter to dub him "Big Play Monteilh." Ron's big plays eventually earned him a scholarship to Oregon State, which he chose over CU. After one year, though, he transferred to Colorado and had to sit out a season of football under the NCAA transfer rules. It would be a year he would never forget. His story would become a real-life imitation of the racial-injustice detailed in Harper Lee's classic novel "To Kill A Mockingbird."

A week after CU won the 2001 Big 12 championship, the lives of many CU players changed in the wake of the now-infamous party at Lisa Simpson's Boulder apartment. Monteilh was one of more than a dozen players who stopped in at the party, but he left prior to the activities that thrust both he and the team into a blinding national spotlight. By the fall of 2004, the events that followed had been well chronicled, at least from the standpoint of the accusers. When Simpson and Anne Gilmore, claimed to have been raped while drunk at the party, no rape charges were filed, but fingers were pointed. District Attorney

Mary Keenan pointed one of those fingers at Monteilh, who was charged with contributing to the delinquency of a minor by bringing a joint of marijuana to the party.

There was only one problem.

Monteilh didn't bring the pot. He was gone from the apartment before the sexual free-for-all that nearly brought down the CU football program even started. Multiple eyewitnesses and a companion backed Monteilh's contention that he was long gone before the trouble started. In spite of that evidence, he would not be exonerated until the player who brought the joint came forward months later. Monteilh was charged after a recruit looked at a media guide and identified him as the one who brought the pot. Monteilh's picture, however, wasn't even in the media guide. It will likely never be known how his name ended up under a picture shown to the recruit.

"He hadn't even taken a football picture because he had to lay out that season," his mother said. "I don't know how he could have been identified. Maybe they put his name under someone else's picture." Solely because of that single piece of obviously poor evidence, Monteilh was charged with a felony. Insult was soon added to injury.

"When the players' pictures appeared in the paper, all the other players had their football pictures published," Marissa said. "Ron hadn't taken a football picture, so they used his police mug shot. It made him look bad."

Marissa said she knew about the party before her son's arrest, but was sure he had done nothing wrong. "Ron told me there were four names out there (under suspicion)," she said. "He had already told me what he knew and what he didn't know, so I didn't ask him again. I followed it in the paper like everyone else."

That would soon change with a phone call from her son.

"Ron called me and said something shady's going on," she said.

His next words nearly dropped her.

"I have to turn myself in."

Up to that point, things had been looking up for Marissa. After self-publishing a novel that was a fictionalized version of her own life story, she had signed a contract with HarperCollins for the re-issue of the book and the publication of another volume of "women's fiction" each year. Her life had turned a big corner, but it looked as though her son was about to go to jail.

She immediately headed for Boulder.

"I drove to Colorado and picked Ron up," she said, "and we drove over for him to turn himself in. We prayed as we got out of the car."

Marissa stayed in Boulder for a few days to attend her son's first court appearance.

"The media was everywhere," she said, "jamming cameras and microphones in our faces. The team was also there. They stood outside and cheered us as we went in the courthouse. They were saying, 'Shoulder to Shoulder, we're here.' "

Marissa was angry when she learned that her son was misidentified and was even angrier that the DA had relied on what she saw as such a flimsy shred of evidence. When she first talked to Barnett on the phone, she was worried that he would revoke her son's scholarship. He had revoked the scholarships of the four players who admitted bringing alcohol or bringing recruits to the party and she was worried that her son could be next. It, however, never came to that.

"He said not to worry, that Ron had told him the truth and had come forward. He had faith in Ron's word," she said. "Gary was the one who was there to talk to me. He listened to me." Marissa said Barnett proved to be the same man she had met when he first recruited her son.

"From the first time Gary Barnett came in my living room, I knew who he was. He talked about the importance of academics and he talked about the challenges of being a minority athlete. I felt very comfortable with him."

After accompanying her son to his initial court appearance, the two went out to breakfast. "We left and went out to breakfast, where we talked for a long time," she said. "We talked about racism and a lot of things."

During that same time period the Monteilh family suffered through the death of several relatives and close friends. There were other bad breaks. During a Christmas-break trip to Los Angeles in December of 2004, Ron got into an accident in which his used car was wrecked. "There were times when I just prayed for a break—for something good to happen in our lives," his mother said.

Barnett was impressed with Marissa's strength and would later call her "one of the strongest people I've ever met." He said, "Her faith was so strong that she knew everything would turn out all right," he said.

It would take a while, however. It would be an act by one of his teammates that would set things straight with the law.

"Months later the guy who did it said he was turning himself in," she said. "I admire him for doing that." That guy was CU defensive back Clyde Surrell, who eventually told police he was the one who brought the joint. It took a confession from Surrell to convince prosecutors that Ron had been misidentified. "Ron got a call (about the dismissal) when he was back here at home," she said. "The charge was dropped, but the name of Ron Monteilh had been tainted. How do you repair that? How do you un-do the damage to his reputation?"

Ron Monteilh would have to repair that damage without the help of the district attorney or the media. Keenan never apologized for the false accusations. The media's response to the dismissal of the charges came only in what Marissa Monteilh called, "one line in one paper."

Marissa said both she and her son relied on their religious faith to get them through the ordeal. "If you wait upon the Lord, your strength will be returned," she said. "Ron knew who he was and we knew who he was. I always taught my kids not to care what anyone else thinks." She said her son doesn't want to be known as someone who has faced challenges or someone who wants others to feel sorry for him.

"He won't tell you that we struggled when he was young," she said. "He won't tell you that we were once evicted and he won't tell you about having to catch the bus to school at 5 a.m. and scraping change together to afford the fare."

Ron Monteilh said a combination of things helped him get through the period when he was accused of being a druggie and, by inference, a rapist.

"What got me through being falsely accused was the strong, unconditional support of my family, faith in God, patience and determination to finish what I came to CU for—to get a degree and play football, in that order. I did that," he said while claiming he doesn't dwell on that period of his life and doesn't carry any grudges.

"No, I don't have animosity," he said. "There was a rush to accuse—I was a victim of that fact. However, I know and accept that challenges are guaranteed in life. You learn from it and move on." Monteilh spent the winter training for a hoped-for career in professional football, but went undrafted and unsigned by the pros. He graduated in May 2005 with a degree in economics.

His mother, however, still bristles at the fact that the media didn't seem to care that her son had been wrongly accused. "No one ever did a story about who Ron really is," she said. "He never went to the papers to get them to clear his name."

He shouldn't have had to go to the papers. Aren't enterprising reporters supposed to uncover injustice and the plight of the wrongfully accused? Reporters' purported empathy with victims doesn't extend to those they victimize themselves.

According to Marissa, the son to whom she taught life's hard lessons ended up teaching her a few things. "I learned about struggle through example," she said. "My son's example."

McChesney, one of Monteilh's closest friends on the team, described the quiet young man in much the same manner. "Ron doesn't care what others think,' he said. "He has always known who he is." McChesney said he was amazed at both Monteilh's strength and calm during that time. "It's a feat Ron can be proud of the rest of his life," he said.

Against Kansas State, Ron Monteilh was looking for more immediate gratification in his last home game. His mother almost didn't make it to that game, but a strange series of events turned the third weekend in November into one neither she nor her son would ever forget.

"I wasn't going to go to that game," she said. "I'd been gone a lot and writers only get paid twice a year. My travel budget was gone, but about three days before the game I found a plane fare on the Internet that was about a quarter of the regular fare. 'Let me grab this,' I said to myself."

After landing in Denver the day before the game, Marissa went to the Omni Interlocken Hotel to visit Ron. When the players retired to their rooms, she went back to her room to get some sleep. That sleep was interrupted in the middle of the night by a strange dream.

"I was having a dream in which I was at the football game," she said. "I was cheering because the team was doing well and I looked to my right and, in the dream, my late husband was sitting there. He told me, 'Ron is about to go deep.' I woke up immediately and started crying. It was 3 a.m."

The next morning Marissa told her son about the dream in which his late father had appeared. "He listened to the story and didn't say anything," she recalled. 'I wasn't sure if I should have told him that story on the morning before a big game, but I did."

If Marissa's dream was surreal, it was no more so that the atmosphere at Folsom Field on Saturday morning. The bundled-up crowd of about 43,000 people arrived slowly and was uncharacteristically quiet. The 12:30 p.m. game was not on TV and the atmosphere didn't feel much like a pivotal Big 12 game, but it was about to become one.

Early on, both the CU and K-State offenses looked as cold as the weather. Each team punted on its first possession before CU got the ball for the second time with just over 11 minutes left in the first quarter. Running back Bobby Purify, who had been battling injuries to both his shoulders and his knee, ran for 35 yards on first down and the Folsom Field crowd started coming to life.

Employing a running game that was starting to look like the one they had ridden to a league championship three years earlier, the Buffs scored on a 1-yard run by quarterback Joel Klatt. Early in the second quarter CU would extend its lead to 10-0 when Monteilh caught a 13-yard pass that took his team to K-State's 33-yard line and which enabled Mason Crosby to kick a 51-yard field goal. It marked the fifth time of the season that Crosby had a field goal longer than 50 yards.

The Buffs' 10-0 lead didn't last long. K-State quarterback Allen Webb, who had been recruited by CU and who was the grandson of longtime Denver Mayor Wellington Webb, drove his team 80 yards on a 14-play drive. Webb carried the ball five times and completed three passes before pre-season Heisman Trophy candidate Darren Sproles scored on a 1-yard run. CU's lead was cut to 10-7. With just over a minute left in the first half,

K-State kicker Joe Rheem got kicked a 52-yard field goal and the game was tied 10-10 at the half. Ron Monteilh had caught two passes, but still had no touchdown.

Although it was not quite the off-the-field break Marissa Monteilh had prayed for, CU finally caught a break early in the third quarter when K-State punt returner Yamon Figurs fumbled a punt on his own 9-yard line. Stephone Robinson, who had been the hero of the Kansas game and who would spend the coming winter wondering who sent him threatening, racist e-mails, played the hero again and recovered the fumble. Robinson, whose mother earlier told reporters that the attacks on the CU football program had forced her son to "quit wearing his CU stuff when he goes to the mall," was in the spotlight for the second week in a row. The Buffs were up 17-10 and were about to add another touchdown.

On CU's next possession wide receiver Bernard Jackson, who had entered the season as a backup quarterback, came into the game as a wide receiver. Klatt handed him the ball on what looked like an end-around running play, but Jackson stopped in the backfield. Just as he was getting leveled, he threw a 41-yard pass to Blake Mackey that put the Buffs in business at the K-State 31-yard line. Three plays later Klatt hit Joe Klopfenstein with a 5-yard touchdown pass and CU had a commanding 24-10 lead.

They wouldn't have it for long. With Allen Webb showing why he was highly recruited after high school, K-State scored a touchdown. Webb's 11-yard touchdown run closed the gap to 24-17. Then disaster struck for CU. Three plays after K-State's score defensive back Ted Sims intercepted a Klatt pass and returned it 32 yards for a touchdown. The game was tied at 24 and Kansas State was on a roll.

CU came back quickly on a series in which Monteilh caught his third pass of the game, a 22-yard completion that gave CU a first down on the K-State 38-yard line. Six plays later Purify scored his second touchdown of the day and CU was up 31-24 with four minutes left in the game. K-State looked to be in real trouble on the next series when Webb was dinged up and left the game. But his replacement, Dylan Meier, came out throwing. His 17-yard touchdown pass to Jermaine Moeiera tied the game at 31 with 30 seconds left in the game. It looked as though CU's only chance to win would be in overtime.

CU had to hurry to at least get in position for a field goal. Klatt threw to wide receiver Mike Duren, but the pass was incomplete and the clock stopped. On second down he threw toward Monteilh, but that pass also fell to the ground. On third down Klatt hit Lawrence Vickers with a 13-yard pass that gave CU a first down on its own 36-yard line. The Buffs had the first down they needed to stop the clock, but had only 15 seconds left to score. They weren't even close to field-goal range, even for the strong-legged Crosby.

And they had only one play to get there.

The world went into slow motion for Marissa Monteilh when the ball was snapped. Klatt, under heavy pressure, rolled out. Ron Monteilh kept running his route. Finally Klatt let the ball fly, hitting Monteilh in stride along the left sideline. Monteilh sprinted down the sideline and in to the end zone, coming to rest on the same spot where he and other players had kneeled to pray before the game and at halftime.

Either the Nike-issued knee-high white socks or Marissa Monteilh's unswerving faith had worked.

While not quite considered a miracle, the game-winning play came 20 years after CU's fabled "Miracle in Michigan," in which quarterback Kordell Stewart threw a desperation pass to Michael Westbrook for the game-winning score. Ironically, both plays went for 64 yards. Marissa Monteilh, however, saw her son's catch it as the miracle forecast in her pre-dawn dream.

"I saw that someone caught the ball, but I didn't realize it was Ron in the crowd of players near the sideline, "Marissa said. "Then the lady next to me grabbed my arm and told me it was Ron. He just kept running until he reached the end zone."

Suddenly the bizarre dream Marissa had before the sun rose that day had come true. By her own admission, she went nuts.

"I just lost it," she said. "I basically lost my mind. I started screaming and crying. I was jumping up and down. I thought I was going to need a diaper out there. Words can't explain it. Everything just unfolded the way it was supposed to."

Patty Klopfenstein, the mother of tight end Joe Klopfenstein, was seated behind Marissa Monteilh. "I felt a hand on my shoulder and it was Patty," Marissa said. "I turned around and hugged her. Patty understood what all of this meant to me. She was so good to everyone during all the trouble. I love her so much."

Klopfenstein will probably never forget watching Marissa when her son scored his first touchdown of the year. "Marissa was crying and yelling and trying to call people on her cell phone," she said. "It brought tears to my eyes, too."

It also brought a giant roar from the crowd.

Ron Monteilh was temporarily buried under a pile of celebrating teammates. When he emerged, he looked up at the crowd and held up two fingers on one hand and four fingers on the other to pay homage to his late father.

"That was for number 24," his mother said. "His dad was a wide receiver and wore 24. I cried my eyes out when he did that."

She wasn't the only one.

"I had tears in my eyes and I couldn't breathe," McChesney said after the game. "This was great for Ron and a great ending overall at Folsom Field."

McChesney, who had a bird's-eye view of Monteilh's struggles on and off the field, said he never lost faith in his. "I *can* believe it happened the way it did," he said. "That's why we call him Big Play Monteilh."

Monteilh's catch and run seemed to overshadow the 38-31 win. Lost in the excitement was the fact that the CU offense, which had struggled mightily, scored 38 points against a good opponent. Purify had rushed for 155 yards. The Buffs were 6-4 and eligible for a bowl game. In a post-game interview with sports writers, Ron Monteilh didn't seize the opportunity to lash out at those who had falsely accused him three years earlier. He only talked about the play that won the game.

"I saw (Klatt) scrambling out and I just tried to get to the sideline because no one was there," he said. "At first I was just looking back thinking he had already thrown the ball, but he was looking at me so I kept running to get open. When we first got the ball on the drive I was thinking that we didn't have to get too far to let (kicker) Mason Crosby have a shot. When I caught the ball I was thinking to get out of bounds to give Mason a chance, but they had a breakdown, so I just kept running."

Marissa said her son was matter-of-fact about the catch when she met him outside the locker room after the game. "He just told me, 'You said it was going to happen.' He believed me."

There were no post-game newspaper stories about how Ron Monteilh had overcome false accusations and kept his head held high. Months later the media would remain virtually silent about a series of racially motivated e-mail threats sent to the team in 2004 and to Stephone Robinson in 2005. Those weren't the only instances in which the media failed to follow up on its irresponsible, one-sided stories.

Denver attorney Dan Caplis, who hosts a radio talk show and who once referred to attacks on the CU football team as the acts of a "media lynch mob," said media bias was never more evident than when police rounded up two black football players after a woman reported being drugged and raped by two men she met at a Boulder bar in 2004. In that case the woman only remembered talking to a pair of black men at the bar and could not remember the assault.

DNA tests failed to connect the players to the incident. But that part of the story went almost completely unreported. "That was a shocking story that you expect to read about Birmingham, Alabama, in the 1950s," Caplis said. "Two black football players were singled out, but were innocent. That's a shocking story out of the one of the worst eras in American history and the media should have been outraged. Liberal Boulder should have been outraged."

Caplis said the media's inaction in that story "shows either an anti-football program bias or a racial bias." Calling the incident "a huge, important story" he said it provided "the grossest example of media bias regarding the CU football program."

It could be argued that gender bias also played a role in the media's coverage of the CU situation. When victim advocate Janine D'Anniballe told the Independent Investigative Commission that "two more women" had called her office to report that they had been sexually assaulted by CU football players, she provided only unsubstantiated allegations and no details. For the most part, the media let her do it. Keith Coffman, a veteran Denver reporter who covered the committee hearings for Reuters, recalled what happened when he approached D'Anniballe after the meeting and pressed her for information

"She told me she had no way to verify the allegations," Coffman said, "but it was the first thing she blurted out when she appeared before the committee. It was obvious she said it so that the newspapers would give it big play. And they did." Coffman continued to press D'Anniballe for any details that would substantiate her allegations, but got only a broad-based indictment of men in general. Coffman said she told him "I don't think that football players have a special place in the line of sexual assault. It's men in general."

While D'Anniballe's statement displayed a bias against men, that bias went unchallenged by the committee during her testimony. "They didn't press her on it," Coffman said. "I couldn't believe it."

Coffman also couldn't believe what happened right after he tried to question D'Anniballe. He said Regina Cowles, the head of the Boulder chapter of the National Organization for Women, got in his face for asking questions of D'Anniballe. "Cowles cornered me and started screeching at me for attacking victims," he said. Of course, neither D'Anniballe nor Cowles could identify a single victim, but that didn't seem to matter to reporters interested only in publishing the latest allegations-of-the-day, no matter how nebulous or unfounded they may be.

Those unsubstantiated allegations injured innocent people whose names were sullied by innuendo—people like Ron Monteilh, who had the grace to move on and ignore the false allegations fueled by ignorance, sexism and even racism.

What about Marissa Monteilh, who lived through the hell of her son being labeled a drug distributor or even a rapist? While harboring resentment for a district attorney who needlessly tainted her son's reputation, she now sees the whole incident as a character builder.

"You ask why a thing like that happens," she said. "Perhaps it was to strengthen him, to teach him to have faith and to not give up. Now I know that Ron's evolution was occurring as it was supposed to."

But, she still finds it hard to forget what happened to her son.

"It's hard because you are guilty until proven innocent," she said. "They said that Ron Monteilh, Jr., the son of Ron Monteilh, Sr., was a felon. Would I like to go after them for what they did?

Sure, I would. You're supposed to forgive and forget, but you never forget something like that."

Unfortunately the media found it rather easy.

The CU football players, however, wouldn't find it easy to back up McChesney's brash prediction of a Big 12 North championship. The last game of the season would take the team to Nebraska on the day after Thanksgiving and even a win there would make the Buffs dependent on the outcome of other games in their underdog quest for the division championship.

By the time the team had played 10 of its 11 regular-season games, it was easy to identify its supporters. There were the parents who traveled to as many games as they could. There were a few well-heeled fans who made most of the road trips. Former players scattered about he country would show up on the sidelines in various locations to show their support. Early in the season some two dozens members of coach Gary Barnett's college fraternity had traveled to Boulder for the Oklahoma State game, only to see their longtime friend suffer a lopsided defeat.

But Nebraska was less than a day's drive from Colorado and a large contingent of parents and fans would travel to Lincoln for that last game. With the team now in a position to get its seventh win and shot at the North Division championship, fans not related to the players would make the trip.

While they didn't make the trip, a small, very unlikely group of CU fans some 2,000 miles away would watch the nationally-televised game and root for the Buffs. That group, which had been a little-known but important ally of the team since the Nebraska game three years earlier, had faced challenges much more serious than anything the Buffs had endured.

Chapter Thirteen
From the Darkness

Throughout the 2004 season, CU's coaches and players publicly said they were ignoring the myriad of allegations that had been tossed at them and were solidified by the support of their families and teammates. The phrase, "We know who we really are," had been uttered repeatedly by both coach Gary Barnett and his players.

They knew who their friends were, too.

There were, of course, those fans who formed a tunnel of support outside the team bus before the first game.

But mostly there were the families.

During Family Week, which preceded the Iowa State game, family members had come from as far away as Hawaii. Clifford Dizon, whose son Jordan was a starting linebacker in his freshman year, shivered in the late-afternoon Colorado weather as he watched practice. The older Dizon, who works for a gas-supply company on the island of Kauai, took a week off from work so he could stay in Boulder long enough to see two home games. The trip was a last-minute thing. "I didn't expect to come out there this year because I didn't expect Jordan to play," he said about his trip through four time zones.

Clifford Dizon was joined at the practice by Dan Jolley, an Army combat instructor who had traveled from Texas to see his son, fullback Daniel Jolley. "I'm glad I brought a parka," he said as he shivered along with fellow warm-weather resident Clifford Dizon.

Karen Crosby was more of a fixture in Boulder and knew the drill. She kept moving out of the shade and into the sun while watching that same practice. Her family traveled to most of CU's Buffs games from the family home in Georgetown, Texas.

During Family Week, Karen spent the whole week in Boulder as a house guest in the home rented by her son, kicker Mason Crosby, and his football-player roommates. While visiting she did what she called "a little cooking" and "a lot of cleaning." On Wednesday of that week, her son cooked her a birthday dinner.

The players seemed to have extended fan-families in their hometowns. Residents of Kauai got up early on Saturdays to watch hometown-boy Dizon play on the mainland. Some of those games started as early as 7:30 a.m. in Hawaii.

In Georgetown, a short drive north from Austin, Mason Crosby's games were as popular as the high school games that routinely drew 12,000-15,000 fans in a town with 30,000 residents. The Crosby family usually boasted 12-15 family or community members at CU's road games and about 100 Crosby fans made the relatively-short trip to the Texas A&M game. The exploits of kicker Crosby, who would later be named to the Playboy Pre-Season All-America Team for 2005, were followed closely in his hometown.

"My daddy's in poor health," Karen Crosby said during her Family Week trip to Boulder. "There's a newspaper picture in his hospital room of Mason kicking a long field goal against Colorado State." His grandfather's failing health forced Mason Crosby to make an unscheduled trip back to Texas during the season, but CU coach Gary Barnett had already gotten a taste of the Crosby family's tight-knit nature when he visited the family home to recruit Mason two years earlier. "Everyone was there— grandmothers, grandfathers, aunts and uncles," Karen Crosby said. "There was a large circle of chairs around Coach Barnett. He said it looked like Thanksgiving and asked where the turkey was."

Families like the Crosbys, whose values seemed to resemble those of the Waltons, had seen their sons portrayed as thugs and rapists.

Some of the parents made bigger sacrifices than others in supporting their kids. Defensive end James Garee's parents, Jack and Shirley, drove to every game while Jack battled lung and brain cancer.

The football-parent family was drawn even closer when the recruiting allegations hit full stride in 2004. The Crosbys and the other families took the accusations personally. "Those allegations reflected on us, the parents," Karen Crosby said. "People were wondering how we could send our sons to that place. These are our children and we know better than to send them to a program like that. CU is a place of integrity and these coaches are the ones influencing our sons in the next step of their lives."

Families separated by time zones, culture, religion and race were drawn closer by the controversy and were stitched together by Patty Klopfenstein, the mother of tight end Joe Klopfenstein. She served as the clearing house for an e-mail group that shared on-the-field and off-the-field news about the team. The woman known to the other parents simply as Patty also led the charge when it came to defending the team in public. She organized a press conference, demanded and got an audience with Governor Bill Owens and became the public face of the parents' group.

As the Buffs came down the home stretch of their 2004 season, their supporters included an unlikely group in an unlikely place. While the CU football team travels to Manhattan, Kansas, every other year, few have ever visited the "other Manhattan" in New York, New York. The CU team flag, however, hangs proudly in a building just a few doors from Madison Square Garden and just up the street from the Empire State Building. That building houses a group of CU fans who have followed the team for more than three years and who have battled adversity far worse than anything the CU football program has ever endured.

The building on New York's 31st Street houses the New York City Fire Department's Engine Company 1 and Ladder Company

24, a firehouse that has been nicknamed Midtown Madness and which handles more than 8,000 calls per year. The busiest firehouse in the nation's busiest city stood firmly in CU's corner during the events of 2004, but the allegiance had nothing to do with football. It had everything to do, however, with the events of September 11, 2001, a day during which the New York City firefighters lost 343 of their brethren while saving another 25,000 people from death in the fireballs that were once the World Trade Center Towers.

The unlikely relationship between Engine 1-Ladder 24 and the CU football team began through happenstance and which was cultivated by mutual respect and adversity.

Engine 1-Ladder-24 didn't get called out when the first airplane struck the World Trade Center. Higher-ups, fearing an imminent attack on the nearby Empire State Building, wanted the company that included E-1/L-24 close to home in case it was needed there. But, when an airliner hit the second tower, all bets were off. The firefighters from Engine 1-Ladder 24 were dispatched to what would later be known as Ground Zero. Some would never return. Among those who died that day was Father Mychal Judge, the FDNY chaplain who lived literally across the street from the Engine 1/Ladder 24. "Father Mike," as he was called, had spent a lot of time at that firehouse and knew all the men. He even performed the Mass at firefighter Jimmy Cody's wedding. Father Mike would also be listed as the first official fire department casualty of the World Trade Center attacks.

For Paul Keogh, the tragedy hit home and hit hard. A CU graduate who had been in the oil business, he lived in New York and knew the men of the E-1/L-24 as friends. In the aftermath of 9-11, they would become much more. While New York City dealt with the deadliest-ever attack on American soil, the rest of the country looked on in disbelief. While his job was to coach the University of Colorado football team, Gary Barnett suffered through the news like every other American. In the days before the terrorist-manned jets hit New York City, the Pentagon and a field in Pennsylvania, Barnett's team was preparing for a Sept. 15 road game against Washington State. That game, along with every other scheduled that weekend, was postponed indefinitely. It would be three years before the game was played—on September 11, 2004.

Not long before the terrorist attacks, Keogh had been a sideline guest of Barnett at a CU game. Within days of the attacks, he sent Barnett a T-shirt and a hat emblazoned with the letters FDNY. When Barnett wore them to practice, his players took note.

"Several of the kids wanted one," he said of the shirts.

Keogh and the men of E-1/L-24 were happy to oblige. Through the efforts of Jimmy Cody, a box of hats and shirts made its way to Boulder. The CU football team and the firefighters had made an accidental connection, but it wouldn't remain accidental for long. Some two months after the terrorist attacks, Barnett invited about a dozen of the firefighters to attend a game in Boulder. Some of the men, including Cody, were working nearly around the clock at Ground Zero and couldn't attend. Those who did changed both their own lives and the lives of the football players they had come to meet.

The firefighters were not the kind of people you would expect to meet in Boulder. Many came from generations of New York firefighters. They were the sons and grandsons of immigrants from Ireland, Poland and Italy. Some were the descendants of slaves. They were Catholics, Protestants and Jews. They were plain-spoken guys who almost always refer to their occupation simply as "the job." Many were the kind of men who might swear at the dinner table and drink to excess on St. Patrick's Day, but who would unflinchingly risk their lives for strangers because that was part of "the job." They call each other by nicknames like Bones, Rhino and Wojo. Unlike the media, most of them weren't much on political correctness. They had neither the time nor the desire to sugarcoat their words, lives or deeds.

One of the trucks at the E-1/L-24 firehouse proudly displays the name of Father Mike and Battalion Chief Thomas Farino, along with the names of five other members of that company who never returned from duty on Sept 11. There was Michael Weinberg, who interrupted a day-off golf game to report for duty from which he would never return. There was Captain Daniel Brethel, who responded during his day off and who, like 342 others, never returned. There was firefighter Steve Belson, whose remains Jimmy Cody would spend eight futile months trying to locate under the rubble of the towers. And there were the names of Lieutenant Andrew Desperito and firefighter Bill Henry. Photographer Laura Yanes, who is currently photographing what she hopes will be the complete roster of all 11,000 FDNY firefighters, said that to this day there is a sense of grief among firefighters "on a scale I can't begin to define."

Paul Keogh saw that grief. He wanted to help his firefighter friends. He wanted them to get away for a while. And he wanted to see the grim-faced heroes of 9-11 smile again. So he paid their way to the CU-Nebraska game that was played on the day after Thanksgiving, little more than six weeks after the death of 343 of their co-workers and brothers. "The events of 9-11 had been horribly rough on them," Keogh said. "I wanted them to have a break."

By all indications, the firefighters had a ball that day. So did the CU football team, which defeated Nebraska 62-36 in what virtually every hardcore CU fan calls the greatest game in school history. The firefighters lined the CU sideline and at halftime began throwing T-shirts into the crowd. They became the stars of the game. CU running back Bobby Purify's father caught one of the shirts and came to the sideline to get it autographed. "By the end of the game they were all laughing and smiling again," Keogh said. "They hadn't smiled since 9-11."

A bond was formed that day between the CU football program and the firefighters, but it would get stronger. When the team won the Big 12 in 2001 and went to the Fiesta Bowl, CU booster Mike Tanner paid for a group of five firefighters to travel to Tempe, Arizona, for the game. Among those attending was Steve Wojciechowski, who was known to his buddies as Wojo and who had been in the group that attended the Nebraska game weeks before. The native New Yorker made quite an impression on the driving range of one of the Phoenix area's most exclusive golf courses.

"Wojo was standing down there hitting balls, dressed in OP shorts, his work boots and a Hawaiian shirt," Tanner said. "A lady told one of the employees there was a strangely-dressed man hitting balls and she was concerned. When she was told he was a New York firefighter, she rushed down there to get her picture taken with him." Wojo, meanwhile, was battling the emotional and physical wounds of Sept. 11. While he remained on the job, many didn't. More than 3,000 FDNY firefighters have retired since Sept. 11, many because of the injury and trauma left by the terrorist attacks. FDNY was also taking it from the tabloids in New York. One story alleged that firefighters had reportedly stolen jeans from a store during the rescue search of the World Trade Center buildings. Cody, a 20-year veteran at the time, has a simple response to those charges.

"You're shittin' me," he remembered thinking when that story came out. "They printed one side of a story because it sounded exciting. It wasn't true, but it was exciting. I guess they sold their papers and made their money." For those of us who worked in the media in Denver and Boulder, that assessment would soon sound very familiar. When Cody agreed to talk with me he said it was his first interview. And his last.

One might have expected the relationship between the football team and the fire fighters to fade when, in early 2002, four CU players were charged with contributing to the delinquency of a minor as a result of the Dec. 7, 2001 party at Lisa Simpson's apartment. When the firefighters read stories about the team's problems, they didn't turn on their new-found friends. The football team didn't forget them, either. When CU played the University of Southern California in a non-league game in September 2002, the firefighters were once again invited. Wojo and many of the same firefighters who had attended the Nebraska game the year before were back. This time Jimmy Cody also made the trip.

Tanner kicked in some of the money to bring the FDNY guys out to Boulder. So did CU booster Tom Welch and CU Alumni Association. And so did Barnett, offensive coordinator Shawn Watson and assistant head coach Brian Cabral. Wojo said the group received a tour of the football facilities and an empty Folsom Field before the game.

"By the time the bus arrived at the stadium with the team, we were really pumped up," Wojo said of that day. "We were like, 'go out there and kick their fuckin' ass.'"

They didn't kick anyone's ass that day, but the Buffs certainly found out something about friendship and loyalty. After absorbing a 40-3 defeat, Barnett and the Buffs were down, but Jimmy Cody was there to pick them up. Upon seeing Barnett and his wife, Mary, outside the locker room, Cody gave them some words of support.

"We're still with you," he said. "We're in this for the long haul." Cody, a plain-spoken, blue-collar guy who had seen Hell up close didn't forget those who had reached out to him and to his brothers in their time of need.

Those words of comfort after the loss weren't Cody's only gift that weekend. During the cleanup at the World Trade Towers, he had used a torch to cut crosses out of a twisted beam from one of the towers. He cut 343 crosses—one for each family of the men fire fighters who had died there—and an additional one for the CU football team. Upon his arrival, he tried to give the cross to Mike Tanner with instructions for Tanner to pass it on to team chaplain Mike Spivey.

"Give this to Spivey," he told Tanner.

"No, you give it to him," Tanner replied.

Not one to garner attention for himself and not an outwardly religious man, Cody told Tanner he wouldn't be at the team chapel service the next morning. Not wanting to take no for an answer, Tanner "ordered" Cody and the rest of the firefighters to meet him in the hotel lobby the next morning at 7. The other firefighters, according to Tanner, said there was "no chance" Cody would show up in the morning to present the cross to Spivey.

"Jimmy was the first one I saw coming down the stairs in the morning," Tanner said. "I was surprised and the other guys were shocked." Cody gathered with the others in a short, informal ceremony during which Spivey was given the cross, but he disappeared before Mass, which is held 30 minutes before the chapel services.

"I think he just went out and had a couple cigarettes during Mass," Tanner said. Cody, who called himself "not really a very religious guy,' returned for the chapel service. The cross, along with a piece of marble from taken from a wall in one of the trade center towers, has traveled with Spivey ever since that day and sits on the pulpit at his weekly pre-game chapel services.

Wojo said his relationship with the CU football program has been a key in his recovery from the aftermath of 9-11, but disagreed with those who call him a hero.

"The real heroes aren't here," he said somberly. "They are dead."

While the media's glossy respectful treatment of the New York firefighters seemed to go out of style rather quickly, 2002 also brought more grief to the CU program. Four players were charged in connection with the Simpson party and the team's defensive coordinator, Tom McMahon, lost his battle with cancer. The team won the Big 12 north that year before losing the Big 12 title game. The team slipped to 5-7 in 2003 and 2004 would bring a series of allegations and investigations that would test the mettle of both the team and the university.

Sources say that during the travails of 2004, the CU administration contacted New York City fire officials and warned them that they may want to cease supporting the embattled CU football program. The firefighters, however, would have none of that. Their concern for and support of the team increased when the heat was turned up.

While CU spent the summer of 2004 sort of defending itself, the New York firefighters looked for ways to show support for the program that had reached out to them. It was then that CU booster Mike Tanner, who had become close friends with the guys from E-1/L-24, spearheaded the production of a poster that cemented the relationship between the two groups. He teamed up with Laura Yanes, whose own relationship with the firefighters began only months before the 9-11 attacks when she stopped to photograph Manhattan firefighter Eddie Mecner as part of an assignment for a photography class. Mecner agreed to the photo, but asked if he could have copy. Yanes, agreed, but told him it would be a while before she would have access to the darkroom at the school where she volunteered. After the 9-11 attacks, she took the photograph to Mecner's fire house, wondering if he had survived 9-11. He had survived. Soon other firefighters asked her to photograph them as a hedge against the mortality they faced each day. By the spring of 2005, Yanes had photographed over 6,500 of the city's firefighters and was planning to finish photographing virtually all of them by early 2006.

The firefighters also insisted on using Yanes to photograph a poster they would present to the CU football team. Turning her apartment into a studio, she shot over 150 frames before hitting on the picture used on the poster. During the summer of 2004 the poster finally took shape. It featured two FDNY helmets flanking a CU football helmet. The cross cut from the remains of the World Trade Center formed the center of the picture. The foreground of the picture featured a piece of glass etched by Jimmy Cody and containing the words, "CU Buffs and FDNY, A True Brotherhood." That jagged piece of glass, measuring only a few inches at its widest part, also came from the wreckage of the twin towers and, according to one of the firefighters, "was one of the biggest pieces of glass recovered."

The bottom of the poster carried a line written by Yanes. It said, "From the Darkness, Champions Emerge."

Barnett presented each member of the team with a copy of the poster, which was termed "The September 11 Award," after the team's 20-12 win over Washington State. That game was played on September 11, 2004, exactly three years after the 9-11 attacks.

It was one of the most moving events of Barnett's career.

"Our relationship with the firefighters was one of those unique things that happen in life," he said. "It just happened naturally. It was unplanned and unscripted."

It was also unpublicized. In fact it was nearly a total secret outside the football program and the E-1/L-24 firehouse. At a time when the CU football program could have used any kind of good publicity, the relationship with the firefighters could have served as a great source of positive headlines. To Barnett's enormous credit, he kept the story quiet.

"As we got to know them the relationship just flourished," Barnett said. "I think we gave them something to root for and they gave us a great perspective on what is really important in life."

CU tackle Sam Wilder, whose helmet was chosen for the poster picture, said he didn't know his scratched-up helmet had been used until the poster was presented to the team.

"It was a great honor for me to have my helmet next to those guys' helmets. I was shocked—it was a complete surprise to me," he said. Wilder said it was the football team, not the firefighters, who benefited most from the relationship. "It puts a lot of things into perspective," he said. "What we went through as a team was nothing compared to what those guys went through." Wilder said he is having the poster framed for display in his parents' home. "It's something I will keep forever," he said.

As they boarded a plane bound for Lincoln, Nebraska, on Thanksgiving Day, Wilder and the other seniors thought about the prospect of beating Nebraska three times in five years, something no CU football alumni could brag about. A win in Lincoln would also give the Buffs their seventh win of the season and keep their conference-title hopes alive.

Football weekends in Nebraska are always centered around the Cornhusker, a hotel within walking distance of Memorial Stadium. Visiting fans and teams make their headquarters there, as do the thousands of Nebraska fans who travel to the home games. The covered parking garage at the Cornhusker has signs that read, "No barbecuing in garage." There were no barbecues, however, at the Cornhusker on Thanksgiving night. The crowded restaurant was busy dishing out turkey dinners, while a group of about 30 CU parents and fans ate Thanksgiving dinner in a private dining room.

After their own private Thanksgiving dinner, the CU players milled around the lobby visiting with family and friends. In spite of the huge dinner, the players still had room for snacks before bedtime. Matt McChesney and James Garee compared tattoos as they ate pizza and sandwiches. McChesney had spent a good deal of time that week and that night talking to his many Nebraska relatives, all of whom predicted doom for CU. He was blunt about what he told his relatives.

"I told them they are gonna lose," he said.

As the team bus made its way to the stadium, I realized I was on my last trip with the kids I had come to root for over the past three months. When the bus arrived, I saw my last dose of fan abuse. As Barnett and I walked toward the locker room, a group of women chanted "No Means No." Other fans hooted and hollered as a member of the Nebraska staff summoned two police officers.

"Could you escort Coach Barnett to the locker room?" he asked the two cops. Barnett needed a police escort in hostile stadiums, but it didn't seem to bother him.

"How do you put up with all this?" I asked him as we walked toward the locker room.

"I'd be surprised if it were any different," he said, smiling as though he actually enjoyed the vitriolic atmosphere.

The team seemed loose and confident. The year they had endured seemed to have made them oblivious to the hostility around them.

On the field, the Buffs had their way with the Cornhuskers early. CU jumped to a 10-0 lead in the first quarter and increased the lead to 17-0 early in the second quarter when Bobby Purify scored on a 9-yard run. Nebraska quarterback Joe Dailey narrowed the lead to 17-7 when he scored on a short run with six minutes left in the first half, but CU extended its lead to 20-7 when Mason Crosby kicked a 39-yard field goal as the half ended. CU had Nebraska on the ropes and was in a position to beat the Cornhuskers for the third time in five years.

As the team jogged under the stadium on the way to the visitors' locker room at halftime, the CU coaches kept coaching. Defensive line coach Chris Wilson was animated as he jogged along side his players.

"Do not let fuckers up," he screamed. "Keep up the intensity. Do not let them up."

He needn't have worried.

CU opened the second half with another field goal and added another to take a 26-7 lead as the fourth quarter began. Nebraska put on a furious late comeback, but it was too late. Two Nebraska touchdowns narrowed the lead to 26-20, but when CU got he ball with 1:44 left in the game there was no drama left. Klatt took a knee three times to end the game.

During that last minute, the finality of the situation finally hit me hard. I turned and looked around the stadium one last time. My knees nearly buckled as I gazed around the stadium and realized the things that were ending.

I had already decided to quit my job.

I would soon move away from Denver, my favorite place in the world.

I was about to leave my job, my career and a lot of friends— many on that field. The Nebraska fans displayed a lot of class as the game ended, clapping as the victorious CU players ran off the field. I jogged off the field slowly, trying to milk a few more seconds out of the experience that had changed the way I looked at journalism and the media.

Inside the CU locker room, everyone seemed happy.

Everyone but me.

While I was happy to see what the players had accomplished during what was undoubtedly the most difficult season in school history, I felt lost and alone. The team would go on to play Oklahoma for the Big 12 Championship—a game they would lose—and they would play Texas-El Paso in the Houston Bowl—a game they would win. My assignment with the team was about over and I wouldn't be at either of those games. But, it didn't really matter to me. I realized that I was rooting not for the football team, but for those kids. At that point the football side of things didn't mean much to me. None of this stuff is about football, I thought. It's about the effects of media-fueled attacks on innocent, decent people.

As the coaches emerged from the showers at Nebraska, I mentioned the improbability of the team's late-season success to offensive line coach Dave Borberly. "It only looked like that to outsiders," he said.

Barnett was just as defiant, saying he knew what his team could accomplish but confessing to some doubts along the way.

"I never doubted what this team could do," he said, "but at times I wondered *how* it was going to happen." He did, however, admit to some doubt "after we got behind 14-0 at Kansas."

Outside the visitors' locker room at Nebraska, parents and fans gathered to greet the players. When I walked out of the locker room and saw the joy in their faces, I knew why they were all smiling. It had as much to do with perseverance as it did football. The emotion was too much for me and I slipped away under the stadium and cried like a lost child. In the three months I had been with the team, those kids and their coaches had changed my life in ways they would never realize. I would never see most of them again.

Back in Boulder, the media was suddenly and temporarily back in Barnett's corner. When Missouri beat Iowa State the day after the CU-Nebraska game, the Buffs became the Big 12 North champions. Barnett was selected by the Associated Press as the Big 12 North Coach of the Year. Redemption seemed at hand for the CU football program, but appearances can be deceiving.

In the spring of 2005 the calls for Barnett's firing continued, with the national media once again parroting the biased agenda of the Denver-Boulder media. Meanwhile, across the country criminal charges against football players continued to top the sports pages but failed to ignite the hatred that had been directed at CU. A Southern California cornerback was charged with rape and an Arizona State running back was charged with first-degree murder in the same week, but the national outcry directed at CU was missing. ESPN reporters spent the spring of 2005 knocking on doors in Boulder looking for more female victims of sexual abuse by the CU football team. Perhaps they should have sent some reporters to Los Angeles or Tempe, where the coaches, unlike Gary Barnett, are apparently not being held responsible by the media for every off-field action of their players.

On March 31, 2005 the CU football program got perhaps the best news it had received in years when U.S. District Judge Robert Blackburn dismissed the Simpson-Gilmore case. In his ruling he said the case failed to meet the two standards required in Title 9 cases. Blackburn ruled that the plaintiffs failed to show the university had "actual knowledge" of the alleged sexual harassment and had failed to show the school acted with "deliberate indifference" when it became aware of problems. The lawsuit that looked so juicy in the newspapers with its unsubstantiated allegations had fallen on its face in a court room. The Simpson legal-public relations team had done a masterful job of trying the case in the court of public opinion, but their case had fallen short legally.

While CU officials were jubilant, a terse statement from Simpson's lawyers hinted of an appeal of Blackburn's ruling.

"We disagree with today's ruling," the Simpson team's statement said. "We are concerned the court did not have critical evidence before it in its decision. We are meeting and evaluating our options. Lisa is disappointed with the ruling, but she is committed to having her day in court."

A week later Simpson and Gilmore's lawyers made good on their promise and appealed the dismissal ruling.

Attorneys experienced in the federal courts said it will take more than a year for a decision to come down. If Blackburn's ruling is overturned on appeal, it would likely take another year before a trial could be held. But Blackburn's ruling made the suit look more like what I had slowly come to see it as—an attempted shakedown of the university in which the lawyers thought they could force a lucrative settlement with a barrage of bad publicity and allegations. If that was their plan, it backfired miserably.

By the time Blackburn dismissed the suit, CU had already spent over $1.5 million defending itself. The university could be in a position to recover a fraction of that sum, perhaps as much as $200,000, in costs associated with the case, but will never recover the more than $1 million it spent on legal fees.

A CU press release politely praised the ruling, saying it "supports what we have always known, that this university has never acted with indifference toward its students."
Privately, CU officials were much more blunt.

"This never was about Title 9," said one official who asked that he not be named. "It was a slanderous, baseless attempt to destroy the football program and squeeze a settlement out of the university."

After getting to know dozens of people connected with the CU football program and after spending thousands of hours interviewing hundreds of people while investigating the "recruiting scandal," I found out a lot of things.

I found that the CU program was a loosely-controlled ship when Barnett took over in 1999 and found that he immediately tightened the reigns of discipline. After the ill-fated party in

December of 2001, he moved both swiftly and harshly in punishing players who had violated either the law or team rules. Since then the rules regarding both recruiting and player conduct have gotten even tighter.

Earlier curfews were instituted for visiting recruits.

Recruits were not allowed to be chaperoned by players if not accompanied by coaches.

Academic standards were applied more stringently.

If there was a time when CU football players could conduct themselves in any way they wanted without consequence, that time has clearly been over for a while.

The financial workings of Barnett's football camps have been scrutinized by a private auditor whose nebulous findings were later leaked to reporters who have no idea what a slush fund actually is. Barnett has turned over the records of those same football camps, which are financially identical to ones conducted on nearly every Division 1 campus, to the Colorado State Auditor. The IRS, in the wake of massive and misleading publicity, has also begun auditing the records. Organized crime figures have been subjected to less scrutiny than Barnett has endured. Politicians such as Boulder District Attorney Mary Keenan and Colorado Governor Bill Owens, meanwhile, seem to have escaped media scrutiny entirely.

The most disturbing discoveries I made over the past two years concerned not Barnett or his football program but the media—the members of my own chosen profession who have a failed in their responsibility to be thorough, balanced or anything close to fair. Just before the press conference the day after the 2004 Nebraska game, I ran into CU sports information director David Plati, who pointed out what he saw as the hypocrisy of the media. He made an interesting, yet telling observation.

"In my 20-plus years of traveling around the country, I have seen more drug use, alcohol abuse and infidelity among some in the media than in any other group," Plati told me. Having spent more than two decades in the business, I couldn't argue with his point.

Boulder Daily Camera sports columnist Neil Woelk, who has never been a Gary Barnett supporter, nailed the nature of the so-called CU scandal during a conversation we had in March of 2005. "Fiction has come to be the truth because it's been written so many times," he said.

That fiction has so far hurt a lot of people. What about the families of the players enduring the abuse they have seen heaped on their sons. And what about electrician Jack Garee, who traveled to all those road games knowing they would be the last he saw? Jack died in March of 2005 and didn't live long enough to see his son play his senior year or long enough to see the taint of the broad brush of guilt removed from his family name.

The media's conduct can be attacked more on what was not reported than on what was reported. Allegations of sex assault against young black men have been assumed factual while evidence cutting in the other direction has gone ignored. Hate crimes committed against black CU football players have gone unreported and, even more disturbingly, have gone uninvestigated. The role of Lisa Simpson's press agent in trying her case in the media has also been ignored by reporters who have allowed themselves to be led around by the nose by that same press agent.

Coverage of the "recruiting scandal" at the University of Colorado has been nothing short of a travesty. Opportunistic politicians and lawyers made lap dogs of reporters who fell in step without so much as a whimper when political correctness hijacked factual correctness and racism and sexism hijacked feminism. Thankfully the ill-intended publicity campaign that rocked CU did not also hijack the federal court, which saw through the grandstanding and declared the suit legally unsound.

Blaming the media is very often the refuge of the desperate, but in this case the criticism is right on the money. The coverage of the CU situation has underscored the widespread view of college football players as faceless animals whose purpose is to entertain us for three hours on Saturday.

Free speech guarantees the media's freedom to be irresponsible. It's one of the unavoidable costs of a free society, but media mistakes can and do hurt innocent people. The situation is, indeed, strikingly similar to that portrayed in "Absence of Malice," one of the most thoughtful movies ever made about journalism. In one of the last scenes that movie, Paul Newman's character, who had been wrongfully accused by a reporter of involvement in a murder plot, noted that a woman committed suicide because of the baseless allegations. He asked, "Who do I see about that?"

The answer was nobody.

In "Absence of Malice," art imitated life.

Who do the CU players see about the lies that were written and broadcast?

The answer is nobody.

The public has no control over what is written, but every one of us has control over what we buy, read and watch. No one is forced to buy newspapers or to listen to news broadcasts. It's been said that newspapers are dieing. If that is true, this story goes a long way in explaining why. Americans must become much more critical of what they read, hear and see in the media. If newspapers don't want to tell the unvarnished truth, they deserve such a fate. The electronic media finds itself in the same sinking boat of public distrust, and deserves to be there.

Right now, however, the media's irresponsibility seems to be winning the battle for the mind of the public.

And that is scary.

A thorough examination of the sordid CU story reveals there never was a real recruiting scandal. There was a however, a lot of scandalous behavior on the part of lawyers, press agents and politicians, not to mention unforgivable ineptitude. While no one has yet to prove they are anything but decent human beings, the players and coaches at CU have lived—and will be forced to live—with a series of unsubstantiated allegations for the rest of their lives. The court of public opinion that jumped to convict CU in the Simpson-Gilmore case will not soon reverse itself. Recovering one's reputation is, unfortunately, harder than recovering legal costs.

For the real victims of this racist, sexist jihad, there is no rest.

The past three years have seen a small band of activists armed with a self-serving agenda shamefully buffalo the media and the public that left innocent victims in its wake.

Who do we see about that?